CHANNEL 4

THE SUNDAY TIMES

100 GREATEST
TV ADS

First published in Great Britain in 2000 by HarperCollins

an imprint of HarperCollins*Publishers*

77–85 Fulham Palace Road

London W6 8JB

www.**fire**and**water**.com

Design: Neal Townsend for Essential Books

Picture research: Ruth Hawkins for Essential Books

The right of Mark Robinson to be identified as the author of this work has been asserted by him in accordance with the Copyright, Designs and Patents Act 1988.

10 9 8 7 6 5 4 3 2 1

The Sunday Times is a registered trademark of Times Newspapers Limited.

This book accompanies the TV series produced by Yorkshire Television Limited for Channel 4.

Printed and bound by Bath Press, UK

A catalogue record for this book is available from the British Library

ISBN 0 00 711123 1

CHANNEL 4

THE SUNDAY TIMES

100 GREATEST
TV ADS

MARK ROBINSON

HarperCollins*Publishers*

For Jacob

ACKNOWLEDGMENTS

This book would not have been possible without the work of my colleagues at Yorkshire Tyne Tees Television who made *The 100 Greatest TV Ads* for Channel Four. They include: Peter A. Gordon, Camilla Wheeler, Peter Telford, Martyn Smith, Nickie Lister, Andy Beckett, Yvette Lyons and Andy Matthews. Thanks also to Bridget Boseley and John Whiston, and to Sue Murphy at Channel Four for making it all happen – despite the fact she didn't think the Shackleton's High Seat Chair ad was that funny.

Additional gratitude to all the members of my family (especially Karen, Gabriel and Noah) who have had to endure months of me humming theme tunes ad nauseum from such advertising campaigns as the Milky Bar Kid and R White's Lemonade.

A big 'thanks' to all the people who were interviewed for the programme and whose words have ended up in this book; also to the advertising agencies responsible for working on these 100 campaigns.

Finally, I'm also grateful to John Webster, John Salmon and Bernard Barnett who answered a lot of questions at the start of this project when I naively thought that the Hofmeister Bear was played by a real bear called Hercules. (In fact, it was a Hungarian dwarf called Ivan – but I was close.)

INTRODUCTION

Channel Four had just broadcast our programme *The 100 Greatest TV Moments*. It took up an entire Saturday night; three hours of unforgettable words and pictures from sitcoms, dramas, documentaries, and news and sport events, with commentaries from the people who made them. The programme had been a ratings success. Indeed, the whole '100 Greatest' format seemed to be a winner in a millennium state of 'listeria', but the big question was '*What next?*'.

We submitted a long list of ideas to the commissioning editors at Channel Four – and their verdict surprised me. '*The 100 Greatest TV Ads*?' I exclaimed to my boss, adding (with a startling lack of instinct), 'Would anyone *really* want to sit and watch *ads* for three hours?' Indeed, how would the viewing public react to such a proposition? Would it all end in tears and the longest surge of electricity ever recorded in Britain, as a confused nation boiled the kettle all night? Of all the subjects we had suggested, TV advertising was the one we knew the least about. I should have realised that was its appeal. After all, we had grown up with the Smash Martians, and ads for Levi's 501s and Carling Black Label, but we knew precisely nothing about the stories behind these TV moments, as instantly recognisable as any scene from a sitcom or denouement from a drama.

There were so many questions: How did campaigns like these come about? Who were these unknown, unfeted people who created them? And whatever led the admen to put Henry Cooper and Kevin Keegan in a shower for a Brut commercial? Over the next few months the members of the production team became immersed in the minutiae of television advertising history. Soon, telephone calls were being exchanged about Elvis Costello's alleged involvement in the history of the Secret Lemonade Drinker. But were we the only ones who would be interested in this sort of thing? Apparently not.

We were relieved to find out that, when Channel Four (and sponsor *The Sunday Times*) opened up their websites and asked viewers to vote on *The 100 Greatest TV Ads,* over 10,000 people did so – more than the number of votes cast in some by-elections. Over the course of several months we spoke to around 100 people who had been involved in the making of the most popular TV commercials ever shown in this country. We ended up interviewing on camera nearly 50 of them – including dozens of actors, writers and directors.

The result was a three-hour programme on a Bank Holiday Monday night in April 2000 that was not so much a history of television advertising as a celebration of famous campaigns and individual ads which had become lodged in our collective memories. So, did anyone *really* want to sit and watch TV commercials for three hours?

Fortunately, they did. The programme pulled in 4 million viewers. In fact, at one point in the evening, there were more people watching old ads on Channel Four than were watching any other channel.

It all goes to show that despite the timeless gags about sticking the kettle on in the break and nipping to the loo, Britain is indeed a nation of ad lovers.

Mark Robinson

100 STORK SB
TELL THE DIFFERENCE 1962

The 'vox pop' is a journalistic practice which costs little and fills a lot of space. No surprise, then, that the streets of Britain are now packed with camera crews tripping up over each other's cables whilst demanding ordinary people give their views on anything and everything.

The idea of challenging the public in this way was popularised by the BBC TV show *Tonight,* which was essential early-evening viewing in the fifties. It featured reporters like Fyfe Robertson who were given the job of going out into the street to vox pop the public on topical issues.

Stork SB was the first advertisement to exploit the genre and one of the first to make the public the stars of its ads. The campaign started off with ads built around 'respectable' people. 'Roy can really handle a plane...but he can't tell Stork from butter,' came the voice-over of a typical early sixties ad. Roy was a crop-spraying pilot.

A decade on, Stork moved operations to where the people actually bought their margarine – the supermarket. *Crackerjack* and *Black and White Minstrels* star Leslie Crowther was the first to ask Britain's shoppers to take the 'Stork Challenge'. But *could* they tell Stork from butter? SB ('Special Blend') or not SB – *that* was the question. 'Leslie Crowther went into supermarkets and started chatting up women about their margarine – a pretty bizarre thing to do if you think about it,' says Rupert Howell, president of the Institute of Practitioners in Advertising. 'It hadn't really been done before, but the problem is now you have a more cynical audience and the first question that would go through people's heads is "How much were these people [the shoppers] paid?" I suspect they were paid nothing.' In 1957, two years after Stork's first TV ad, the first 'Can You Tell The Difference?' campaign began, claiming that four people in five really couldn't tell the difference between Stork and butter. By 1960 Stork had a 43 per cent share of the margarine market.

99 PEDIGREE CHUM
TOP BREEDERS 1969

For over 30 years the makers of Pedigree Chum have been telling us how we too can have an award-winning hound just by feeding it a tin of the chunky stuff with its 'solid nourishment'. Countless Crufts winners and their owners have endorsed the product. 'It's a brilliant piece of marketing because even if you've got a scruffy hound from Battersea Dogs Home, your pooch is very special to you...and the notion that you are giving your dog the very best is a very powerful pull,' says Rupert Howell. 'Everybody knows, as soon as the Crufts winner is announced, the next day the ad's going to be there with the winning champion dog, the proud owner and the Pedigree Chum endorsement.'

Pedigree Chum, launched in 1960, was one of many new canned pet food products that appeared at that time. By 1965 the market had grown to £49 million a year – and Pedigree pet foods accounted for half of it. By the turn of the seventies, pets were really getting the luxury treatment. Not only were they eating stuff out of tins (and not just the leftovers from dinner) they even had countless different varieties. It almost made having every inch of your body prodded and probed by a judge worthwhile.

Chum ads gave us Mrs Froggart and her Corgis; Mr Lister and his Yorkshire Terriers; Mrs Coxall and her Poodles. They even gave us Mrs Torbet and her West Highland Terriers. But perhaps the most famous dog owner to advertise Pedigree Chum was Chris Amoo of the pop group The Real Thing. His Afghan won Crufts in 1987 – and he soon felt the inevitable force of an advertising contract with the makers of Pedigree Chum.

However, as successful as the ad campaign has been, a nagging doubt remains as to its relevance to our everyday life. Do pet food ads really reflect the truth? Broadcaster Stuart Maconie doesn't think so. 'What was always amusing about these adverts was that no dog I'd ever met ever looked like these fantastic, bouncing-with-health Airedales,' says Maconie (brought up in Wigan). 'I'd never seen human beings who spoke like this, either. The owners were these incredibly posh people who seemed to live on 600-acre estates in the home counties. I always used to wonder what *crap* breeders recommended, and where *they* all were, eking out a living and giving their dog all sorts of unsuitable food.'

98 MECCANO
BOY IN A MAN'S WORLD 1967

Perhaps surprisingly this is the only commercial for a child's toy to appear in the Top 100 – a feat that not even Buckaroo, Barbie or the unforgettable Evel Knievel Stunt Cycle could manage. The black and white ad features a young boy who is an engineer of the future, according to the ad voice-over. In between doing his physics homework and helping his dad creosote the garden fence, the clever lad has assembled such treasures as a rocket, an aircraft carrier, and (more curiously) a bulldozer – all from a box of Meccano from the local toy store. 'It reminds you of a more innocent age when young lads wanted nothing more sexy and glamorous than to be a civil engineer and drive a bulldozer,' says Maconie again. 'I bet there are a lot of men of a certain age who would say "Now, in my day we had Meccano – what have they got now? They've got Tomb Raider haven't they and the internet and it's not that good."' Whether some screws and bits of plastic *are* as appealing for growing boys as a computer heroine in a tight top is indeed up for debate. What's not in question is that the advertisers obviously believed that budding *female* engineers weren't worth targeting in the late sixties – just one example of how many of these 100 commercials reflect the thinking of the time.

97 CLARK'S SHOES
BLUEPRINT 1976

Created by Neil Godfrey and Tony Brignull of Collett Dickinson Pearce – one of the pioneering ad agencies from the sixties and seventies – the simplicity of this ad ensured a five-year stint on British TV. Clark's had already been going for 150 years when this ad came along – their first product was a pair of slippers called Brown Peters – but no campaign before or since has had the same impact. The commercial features just three

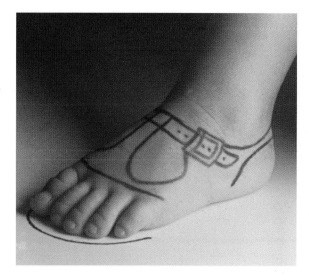

things: a child's foot, an adult's hand and a felt tip pen – which must have meant the props buyer could have the day off.

Over a 40-second period a shoe is drawn on the child's foot to show how Clark's have a child's growth in mind when they design their footwear. 'This little foot will get corns and bunions if a shoe's too tight across here,' intones the announcer at the start of the ad. The ad was shot in the basement of CDP's offices, with Michael Seresin as cameraman. (Seresin would go on to become a top ad director himself, directing among others the Renault Clio Papa/Nicole campaign.) After one child had been picked from several who auditioned for the part of 'Child's Foot In Shoe Ad', it was left to art director Neil Godfrey to draw the outline of the shoe on the said foot. All that was left was a line to leave the public with. 'This is our blueprint' was that line – writer Tony Brignull had been influenced by the fact that Godfrey had drawn with a blue pen. Despite being one of the cheapest ads in this Top 100 (it cost no more than £15,000) the commercial went on to win gold awards in Britain and America. It doesn't take a genius to work out that this ad was very cost effective and one which helped to make the name of Clark's synonymous with children's shoes.

96 SAINSBURY'S
CELEBRITY RECIPES **1991-95**

Viewers are used to seeing celebrities in the kitchen these days. Whenever you turn on daytime and now primetime TV, there seem to be personalities falling over themselves to demonstrate how to be a celebrity and make a *vol-au-vent* at the same time. But *Celebrity Ready Steady Cook* wasn't even on the drawing board when Sainsbury's signed up an impressive collection of British celebs to sell their fresh goods. Over four years in the early nineties TV viewers became used to showbiz stars like Catherine Zeta Jones, Felicity Kendal, Ernie Wise and *Bergerac*

himself, John Nettles, showing how to make their favourite recipes. TV presenter Selina Scott was the first one in the kitchen in May 1991, and Shirley Bassey turned the kitchen lights out and left the washing up till the morning in late 1995.

Perhaps the most unlikely, as well as best remembered, appearance was from the former Labour Chancellor Denis Healey, who finished his preparation of smoked salmon and scrambled eggs by opening a bottle of champagne while stating, 'It really puts the top hat on it.' (This, it was recently revealed, comes from a man who can balance three matchsticks on each eyebrow.

Talent, indeed.). The ads were so popular that, in true Delia Smith fashion (yes, she appeared too), the day after each one appeared on TV Sainsbury's stores were often sold out of products from the previous night's recipe.

95 CHARLIE
BY REVLON **1975**

This Charlie commercial no doubt earned a place in the Top 100 for its perceived role of bringing feminism into TV ad history – and an industry dominated by men. One of the few foreign ads to be selected, the American commercial shows model Shelley Hack driving up to a groovin' jazz bar in a thirties vehicle and making an entrance. Meanwhile, at the piano, cabaret artist Bobby Short sings the virtues of Charlie perfumery: 'There's a fragrance that's here to stay and they call it...Charlie!'

Charlie was launched in 1973 (and in Britain two years later) and saw itself as the first 'lifestyle' fragrance, epitomising the new-found freedom of women across the Western world. After years of TV commercials where glamorous women were seen as sex objects who only wanted to look good for the men in their lives, Charlie set out to be different. For the first time, women were being portrayed as individuals who actually wanted to look good for *themselves*. For the first time, women were wearing the trousers – literally. Charlie set a trend in ads which were to show their aspirational heroine in trousers – and sometimes even a shirt and tie. Women were now seen as expressing their new-found independence – by mimicking men!

Cultural historian Robert Hewison isn't sure that the Charlie ads succeeded in their aim, however: 'The ad says: "With one squirt *you* can wear the trousers. With one squirt, *you* get to drive the smashing car on your own. With one squirt, *you* are in control." But if you look at the ad it's entirely constructed out of men looking at this woman. Although it's saying "You can be free with Charlie," in fact, you are not free because you are in the reassuring web of desire.'

So what happened to the star of the ad, Shelley Hack? Did she become a feminist icon, a symbol of the struggle against male domination? Er, no – she went on to become Tiffany Welles, a member of TV's sexiest crimebusters, Charlie's Angels, when she replaced Kate Jackson in 1980.

94 PARKER PENS
FINISHING SCHOOL 1975

In *The 100 Greatest TV Ads* there are some commercials that took months to conceive and to put into action; and others that were written out of panic, with the admen working round the clock. This ad for a pen called the Parker Lady was one of the latter, as Paul Weiland, who was part of the creative team that thought up the idea, explains: 'Someone had written a commercial for Parker Pens with Una Stubbs in it. It was about an autograph hunter and basically someone walked off with the pen. Well, it was made, but when it was researched it was like: "Hold on, the reason why people don't want to buy expensive pens is because they lose them." The commercial went belly up. There was an air date of the following week and it was panic in the agency.' Over a working lunch at Collett Dickenson Pearce the idea of a finishing school ad came about, in which a teacher gives her young female pupils their final lesson – 'How to spend Daddy's lovely money' – before releasing them into the big, wide world. It was quickly put into production.

Future film director Alan Parker (no relation to the Parker Lady which, in turn, was no relation to Parker, Lady Penelope's chauffeur out of *Thunderbirds*) was brought in to shoot the ad starring Penelope Keith – hot property at the time for her role as stuck-up Margot in *The Good Life*. The British class system was a subject dealt with in the BBC sitcom – after all, Margot did feel superior to everyone else in Surbiton and beyond. And her Parker Pens role was merely a break-time extension. 'Chequebooks open girls,' says the teacher (Keith), 'Pens at the ready.' She then pours scorn on one of the girls for using an improper pen, before her attention is diverted by another pupil. 'Madame, does one spell pence with an 's' or a 'c'?' asks the teenager. 'I don't think you need worry about that dear,' comes the reply.

93 TIMEX
TICK-A-TICK TIMEX **1964**

Timex started out as the Waterbury Clock Company in Conneticut, USA, nearly 150 years ago. Within a decade of changing its name to Timex in 1949, the company was producing the world's bestselling brand of wrist-watch. Timex's American television ads were distinct and innovative. Many featured a 'durability test' presented by a TV reporter called John Cameron Swayze who came up with the slogan 'Takes a licking and keeps on ticking'. Fronting

unedited, news-style reports, Swayze would give running commentaries while the watch was put through a series of 'torture' tests, including being strapped to an outboard motor, a horse's foot and the outside of a barrel thrown over Niagara Falls. In one memorable ad shot in Acapulco, Swayze reports from a cliff top while a high-diving champion behind him – Timex strapped to his wrist – dives into the ocean, then climbs out of the water and walks up to the camera, which witnesses in close-up the still ticking watch. Thanks to ads like these, by the end of the fifties, one in three watches sold in the United States was a Timex. But Timex's British ads were quite different; the company decided the Brits would be more at home with a good jingle – hence the musical sing-song phrase 'Tick-a-Tick Timex'. The words came courtesy of a song called *Good Timin'*, recorded in 1960 by Jimmy Jones – a song which included the phrase 'Ticka ticka time'. All Timex needed to do to come up with a memorable advertising catchphrase was simply add one letter at the end. (They had a 1 in 26 chance of getting it right but did indeed plump for the right letter.)

Over the last 50 years the ad industry has continually used pop music to sell product, whether it be the New Seekers and Coca Cola or Marvin Gaye and Levis 501s. Timex was an early example.

One British Timex ad from the early sixties featured a Beatles look-and-soundalike band, filmed in the famous Cavern Club in Liverpool. The musicians were playing something not unlike a Lennon and McCartney composition, with the all-important phrase 'Tick-a-Tick-Timex' included several times. The ad captured the spirit of the day and helped Timex become as successful in Britain as it was in the United States.

92 GIBBS SR
TINGLING FRESH **1955**

As far as the history of British TV advertising is concerned, *this* is where it all began. ITV was launched on 22 September 1955, and at 8.12pm and seven seconds exactly, around two million viewers witnessed the country's first TV commercial. Dr Charles Hill, who was the Postmaster General at the time, had promised that the ads would not spoil the viewers' entertainment. 'We shall not be bothered by a violinist stopping in the middle of a solo to advise us on his favourite brand of cigarettes. Nor will Hamlet halt his soliloquy to tell us what toothpaste they are using at Elsinore,' he said.

It was during a variety show that compere Jack Jackson introduced the first TV ad saying: 'And now the moment you've all been waiting for, it's time for the commercial break.' The picture cut to a sparkling stream surrounded by snow. To the accompaniment of gentle flute and violin, BBC presenter Alex Mackintosh intoned 'It's tingling fresh, it's fresh as ice, it's Gibbs SR toothpaste.'

One of the two million watching was Brian Palmer, the man who wrote the ad and who (along with everyone else in Britain) was new to television advertising. Palmer had arranged a party at his London home so that his friends who didn't have TV could witness the beginning of commercial television. 'It was complete amazement when the ad came on,' says Palmer. 'We went "That's ours! That's our ad!"' But some of the writer's friends were less impressed. 'I remember my best friend saying "I think you are crazy, Brian – it will never be a major medium."'

Watching critics in Fleet Street agreed. 'I feel neither depraved or uplifted...I've already forgotten the name of the toothpaste,' wrote one journalist. '"Offensive" would be too strong a word by far for these comic little interruptions of the entertainment,' thundered *The Times*.

The Gibbs ad, as Palmer agrees, may have been little more than an illustrated lecture complete with bar chart, but it was a start.

91 BENSON & HEDGES
SMALL CIGARS ISTANBUL **1974**

George Cole has managed to combine a successful career as an actor in TV series and commercials over the past 30 years, though the path hasn't always been smooth. Cole has appeared in popular campaigns for Olympus Cameras and the Leeds Permanent Building Society as well as appearing with Dennis Waterman in nine series of the ITV show *Minder*. But when his role in *Minder* co-incided with a particularly Arthur Daley-esque role in a Leeds commercial, other banks complained. In fact, the role of Arthur Daley was still half a decade away when Cole appeared as a bungling spy in this ad for Benson & Hedges Small Cigars. Set in Istanbul, Cole plays a British secret agent who has planned a rendezvous to pass on some secret missile designs to a Turkish colleague. Believing he has spotted the well-dressed man in question in the midst of a busy market square he offers a cigar to the man with a red carnation in his pocket. However, when this alleged spy lights up his cigar with the rolled-up, top-secret piece of information it becomes clear that Cole has erred. As the wrong man walks away, Cole spots someone identically dressed – right down to the red carnation – coming towards him. (For the sake of national security let's hope someone back home kept a photocopy.) 'What I love about the ad is that it's a beautifully observed piece of humour with the product central to the idea,' says Paul Weiland, one of Britain's top ad writers and directors. 'I think great ads are about where the product is central to the idea, and there would be no commercial without that product.'

The ad was directed by American Bob Brooks who also made the classic Smash Martian ads in the early seventies, as well as the TV sci-fi series *Space 1999*.

9 0 **BARCLAYCARD**
ALAN WHICKER **1984-1988**

Over the past 20 years Barclaycard has used a series of British television personalities to get their message across. Comedy actor Rowan Atkinson played a bungling spy in the nineties, and comedy actor turned presenter Angus Deayton became the face of Barclaycard at the turn of the new millennium. But Alan Whicker came first. Born in 1925, Alan Donald Whicker was a war correspondent in Korea (once reported dead) before joining the BBC's *Tonight* programme in 1957.

Whicker's World, a documentary series in which Whicker did indeed travel the world, started on the BBC two years later then transferred to ITV via Yorkshire Television in the late sixties. Among the most memorable programmes were encounters with American billionaire John Paul Getty and the Haitian dictator Papa Doc Duvalier. By 1970 Whicker had became one of British television's most recognised faces – so much so that Monty Python spoofed *Whicker's World* in a sketch called *Whicker's Island,* where all the inhabitants wore white suits and spent their time looking for rich and famous people to interview. Nearly two decades later, Whicker's Barclaycard campaign would prove a natural commercial extension of a worldwide career in documentaries which saw him travel an estimated three million miles. Indeed, Whicker must have built up considerable air miles during the filming of a dozen ads showing how Barclaycard was (unlike many other credit cards, apparently) acceptable in hundreds of faraway places from Egypt to Italy. (No wonder Whicker lists one of his recreations in *Who's Who* as 'reading airline timetables'.) Rowan Atkinson became the new face of Barclaycard in 1991 in an equally memorable series of ads that also took him around the world. They were made by John Lloyd, who had been Atkinson's producer on *Not The Nine O'Clock News.*

89 CHUNKY
CLEMENT AND HENRY **1967**

They say that people grow to look like their pets (and maybe even the other way round). But the resemblance between TV personality Clement Freud and a bloodhound named Henry was one made in Ad Heaven. In real life, Freud wasn't too keen on a co-star that kept falling asleep on set. Clement Freud was born in 1924, and managed to get a diverse career out of the way before taking part in this series of award-winning ads showing man and his best friend sat side-by-side at the dinner table. After serving in the Second World War Freud was a liaison officer at the Nuremburg War Trials, before training as a chef in Cannes. He was also a sports and cookery writer who became a television personality with an entertainingly downbeat style that endeared him to TV producers and viewers alike. After the campaign had finished it was scandalously revealed that Henry – that lugubrious, hooded-eyed creature – was in fact a female. Freud went on to become a Liberal MP and a *Times* diarist before being knighted in 1987. A St Bernard dog became the new face of Chunky in 1991.

88 DOUBLE DIAMOND
WORKS WONDERS **1968**

Before turning to humour in the late sixties Double Diamond prided itself on TV as 'The Beer The Men Drink'. Its ads showed manly activities like jumping out of a light aircraft at 10,000ft and, having hit the ground, barely stopping for breath before reaching for a pint.

The catchphrase and jingle 'Double Diamond Works Wonders' was to prove a more inventive and humorous way of getting through to its customers. Instead of showing men seemingly willing to lay down their lives for a pint, the ads showed how Double Diamond really could improve your performance (well, in advertising theory, anyway). However, the ad men weren't allowed to claim (unlike those who had worked for Guinness decades earlier) that Double Diamond was 'good for you' – so they had to come up with something cleverer instead. The answer seemed to be setting an ad campaign in the sort of pub which could be seen in any British town or village. Set to the sound of a colliery band trombone, the commercials showed beer-drinking men throwing wayward darts which would, as if by magic, end up as bullseyes... or a pool player who would clear the table with one single shot. It was a clever premise that would be repeated again and again in other TV commercials.

'Beer advertising has a history of what they call transformation – Double Diamond Works Wonders, Heineken Refreshes the Parts, I Bet He Drinks Carling Black Label, and so on,' says Rupert Howell, president of the Institute of Practitioners in Advertisers. 'You drink the beer and something miraculous happens. That's done because the code forbids you from saying: "Drinking alcohol enhances your mood." So what therefore has to happen is you have gentle transformations and these huge humorous exaggerations.'

87 STRAND
YOU'RE NEVER ALONE WITH 1960

Not all of the commercials in *The 100 Greatest TV Ads* were fantastic successes that both charmed the viewers and moved caseloads of the product. Nearly everyone of a certain age remembers the striking Strand commercials, but Strand is an example of a pioneering ad (selling mood instead of brand) which really didn't do the client very much good.

It all began one cold, foggy night in 1960. The ad makers took young actor Terence Brook down to Australia House in London, dressed him up in a raincoat and a trilby to make him look like Frank Sinatra in the film *Pal Joey*, and filmed him outside, smoking a cigarette. 'You're never alone with a Strand,' came the voice-over at the end of the ad. So far so good. Except when Strand cigarettes failed to sell in the numbers expected. Why weren't Strand cigarettes, with their new-look, flick-top pack, selling in their droves? 'The post mortem's conclusion was that people missed the message,' says psychologist Dr David Lewis. 'The message was: "You're never alone with a Strand", but they saw it as, "You're *always* alone with a Strand." People didn't want to step out of their social group and they certainly didn't want to be seen as loners.'

Terence Brook went back to stage acting after his stint as The Lonely Man. Cliff Adams, who was to become one of the country's top jingle writers, responsible for tunes such as 'For Mash Get Smash', wrote *The Lonely Man Theme* for the Strand commercial. 'The ad had only been out for a few days and it got so much comment, I thought, "there's something really big here",' he remembers. 'This was in the days before commercials were transferred into the pop market. This was the first one. I went into the studio and did a three-minute version of it. There was a disc jockey called Jack Jackson who had a Sunday show on BBC radio and he played it. Within 48 hours the thing was a hit.' *The Lonely Man Theme* reached Number 39 in the British singles chart in March 1960.

86 NIMBLE
BALLOON 1968

The owners of hot air balloons must have been falling out of their baskets with mirth in the early seventies. Their services seem to have been required on a regular basis by the makers of British TV commercials. Slimcea bread, Martini and Nimble were all among the products whose advertising campaigns came in a basket in the early seventies. Hot air ballooning conveyed the sense of adventure of the time. In the thrilling years of the Swinging Sixties these characters would have been driving around London in an open-top car. Emily Jones was the original Nimble girl and spent the years 1967 to 1975 munching away on a Nimble sandwich ('only 40 calories a slice!') to the tune of *I Can't Let Maggie Go*. In doing so she became one of the most well-known faces in UK advertising, after an unusual audition with several other would-be balloon girls. 'They got us all into a hot air balloon to see who could cope the best – and apparently it was me,' she recalls. The theme song went on to become a Top Ten hit for Honeybus in 1968, but seven years later Emily Jones bailed out, turned down all sorts of showbiz offers and went to live in Shropshire, where she now runs a bed and breakfast business and hand paints china.

ecipes with Nimble bread.

So many diets are based on substitutes for proper food. Nimble is delicious, real fresh bread, but bread baked lighter so it's designed to fit neatly into a calorie-controlled diet—and so to help you slim.
But because Nimble tastes so good, it's bread that the whole family will enjoy—especially toasted for breakfast—yet one slice of Nimble contains only 40 calories, compared to 67 for ordinary bread.

is a lovely way to slim

Miss Jones had also been the star of other ads, including Fry's Turkish Delight, where she was whipped up on to the horse of a Sheikh who was about to behead her until he discovered she had a supply of chocolate. Lucky for her, eh? Two other Nimble girls have had a slice of the action since Emily Jones. In the eighties South African model Karin Woods executed a perfect dive into a river in a Nimble ad, while ten years later Dutch model Marielle Kruis bungee-jumped out of the same balloon to an updated version of *I Can't Let Maggie Go*. Or rather, that was what the viewer was led to believe. In fact, Kruis's 'death defying' jump was performed in a studio – a ten-foot drop into an airbag. 'Times have changed – and so has Nimble,' ran the voice-over. But the makers of Nimble weren't altogether willing to cut their links with the past. The same ad saw the original 'balloon girl' Emily Jones make a brief guest appearance wearing the same flowing white dress she'd worn 30 years earlier.

85 COURAGE BEST
GERTCHA 1979

Rarely in British advertising has such an eclectic mix of artistry been involved in one 30-second spot. Take the cinematographer on classic films like *Brief Encounter,* add the creator of the Sugar Puffs' Honey Monster, and then sprinkle with the sounds of 'Rockney' pop stars Chas 'n' Dave. The creative force behind the ad was John Webster, who

became known as 'the adman's adman' for his work for agency Boase Massimi Pollitt in the seventies and eighties. 'We were trying to sell Courage Best as a traditional old beer, just like it was in the thirties, with old caps and spit and sawdust on the floor,' says Webster. The inspiration for the ad came via Webster's writing partner Dave Trott, who had just spent the evening in a pub on the Isle of Dogs. 'He came back the next morning with a tape of these pub entertainers called Chas 'n' Dave. It sounded like really traditional pub stuff and dead right. We decided to take the song "Gertcha" and turn it into an ad.' There was one problem – the song was too slow. Webster asked Chas 'n' Dave whether they'd mind playing it twice as fast. It was good advice – the song got into the charts off the back of the ad campaign and launched the Cockney duo's career.

Webster took the phrase, used by Cockneys to express disapproval, and adapted it so that it disapproved of anything that wasn't Courage Best, i.e 'Funny glasses with a little piece of ice – gertcha! Anything that comes with lemon in a slice – gertcha!' Hugh Hudson, director of films like *Chariots of Fire* was brought in to direct. Having decided that the ad should be black and white, Webster and Hudson persuaded Robert Krasker, who had shot films such as *The Third Man*, to come out of retirement and add a touch of authenticity. 'When I arrived on the set, I thought it was awful. Every person had about ten shadows about them,' says Webster. Hudson also had early misgivings: 'Robert had never made an ad before and he was very slow because he was lighting in the old fashioned way.' It was worth it though. 'When we saw it in black and white it looked fantastic.'

84 BRUT
HENRY COOPER **1976**

'Can there ever have been a more homo-erotic 40 seconds in the history of British television?' asks writer and broadcaster Stuart Maconie. 'There's a lot of towel flicking; there's a lot of uncomfortable-looking joshing with each other and knocking each other about. It's a boiling sea of homo-eroticism. I can't believe it got passed.' Maconie is referring to the now infamous ad featuring two of Britain's greatest ever sporting heroes – boxer Henry Cooper and footballer Kevin Keegan. The Cooper/Keegan ad for Brut deodorant was shot in a gym and showed the two stars playing head tennis and indulging in general keep fit before emerging from a steaming shower. It was just one of a number of mid-seventies ads starring the affable Cooper, who single-handedly turned on its head the view that smelling nice made a man a bit of a big girl's blouse. Cooper's other partners-in-Brut included motor racing pin-up Barry Sheene, Olympic gold medallist Daley Thompson and show-jumper (and one time *World of Sport* wrestler) Harvey Smith. It all meant that, as well as being famous for knocking down the then Cassius Clay in the early sixties, Henry Cooper was soon to conjure up other images in the mind of the public – namely a bare-chested man with a squashed nose putting on aftershave while advising us to 'Splash it all over'. However, Cooper wasn't the first sportsman to endorse products. As far back as the early sixties, footballer Jimmy Hill, for instance, was extolling the virtues of using a Remington shaver. (They picked the man with the right chin for the job – plenty of opportunity for facial hair.) But the former heavyweight boxer was perhaps the first sportsman to inject self-deprecating humour into his ad appearances. Gary Lineker has a lot to thank Our 'Enry for. Cooper made his final appearance in a Brut ad in 1988, during which he seemed to be handing over the secret of smelling sweetly to Britain's youth. 'I hope you're not nicking my Brut,' growls Henry when a teenager gets into the bathroom before him. 'No chance, I've got my own,' says the Walkman-clad youth. Brut was moving on. Even Gazza was to have a brief stint endorsing the product.

83 COINTREAU
CATHERINE AND CHRISTIAN 1972

'What *is* Cointreau?' The question was first asked of a small, smouldering Frenchman (not unlike Charles Aznavour) by a rather sophisticated lady at the sort of dinner party where you'd expect the After Eights to be on permanent stand-by.

Out of this one seemingly innocent question there developed a 16-year Anglo-French relationship which was to draw to a romantic conclusion just as its advertising successors, the Gold Blend Couple, were getting steamy around the kettle for the first time. In the early seventies Cointreau hit upon the idea of creating a couple who got it together around the dinner table during a discussion about the ingredients of Cointreau. The couple were played by Christian Toma (now thought to be a teacher) and actress Jennifer Clulow. In the first ad, Christian, who apparently was meant to represent the warmth of the liqueur, launches into a dreamy explanation of how Cointreau is made, right down to the inclusion of 'horranges' – whatever they are. The description is so spellbinding that by the end of the first ad Christian has entranced not only Catherine, but everyone else around the dinner table, who are now listening in deafening silence – a kind of advertising equivalent of Eric Cantona's famous 'Sardines' retirement press conference. Anyway, in half a dozen ads over the next 16 years, viewers saw the romance develop so that by the end of the campaign marriage was on the cards for this long-distance relationship which had helped sell a million litres of Cointreau a year in the UK. In truth, there had to be a French connection to any ad campaign for Cointreau. The drink was created by two brothers in France in the 19th century. A century and a half later Cointreau was selling 13 million bottles a year. Perhaps it's no surprise that Cointreau pioneered, in the soap-style love saga, a new genre of television advertising; way back in 1898 the company was among the first to commission a cinema commercial.

82 SHELL
WE'RE GOING SHELL 1962

In the early days of TV advertising, British ad makers tended to be almost apologetic about taking up viewers' time when they could be watching something that felt far less common and downright *American*.

Long before McDonalds and The Osmonds, TV ads were another piece of *Americana* which some felt would be better left over there. To put it bluntly, having sales people in one's home trying to sell you goods simply wasn't *British*. 'Television advertising seemed very new and very strange and rather American,' says writer Fay Weldon, who worked as an advertising copywriter in the early sixties. 'It seemed a great pity that we were going to have to pay for watching television programmes by having to put up with advertising and somehow the feeling was that it wasn't quite for you.' Ad agencies in the USA had no great dilemmas about how to approach the viewing public. It was all *sell, sell, sell* – their viewers expected it. But that simply wouldn't do in the UK. The advertisers had to be more subtle than that. In short, they couldn't do sell, sell, sell with Shell, Shell, Shell. The result was ads that looked more like a gentle travelogue, and a forerunner of Frank and Nesta Bough touring the world in a holiday show, than a TV commercial. In the fifties, poet John Betjeman was the voice of Shell – taking the viewers on tours of his favourite British towns and villages – and not a petrol station in sight. In the early sixties, this style of advertising evolved into a 'touring musical'. Over the course of 60 *feel-good* musical seconds (with Bing Crosby singing 'We're going well, we're going Shell, you can be sure of Shell') the ad takes the viewer on a driver's eye trip around Britain and 'the Emerald Isles' – from the Tower of London to the lochs of Scotland – a scene unspoilt by motorways or traffic jams. Road rage is a million miles away, as are any shots of petrol going into petrol tanks. The message was clear: Shell petrol gives you freedom – to explore the country if you live in the city, and the city if you live in the country.

81 FRUIT GUMS
DON'T FORGET THE FRUIT GUMS, MUM 1956

Perhaps the first real example of 'pester power' in British advertising, Rowntrees Fruit Gums proved an early victim of the television advertising censors. Early Fruit Gums ads showed earnest, short-trousered school boys following their mother down the garden path as she departs, shopping bag in hand, to the corner shop. 'Bring me back some Fruit Gums, mum.'

'Don't forget the Fruit Gums mum,' we hear the little boy thinking aloud as she walks down the street. (The song, incidentally, wasn't sung by the Aled Jones of the day but Denise Bryer – Nicholas Parsons' wife – who voiced several ads during the fifties and sixties). '"Don't forget the Fruit Gums, mum" would not be allowed nowadays because it is specifically against the codes that forbid the encouragement of pestering,' says Rupert Howell, president of the Institute of Practitioners in Advertising. 'But in those days it was a very innocent sort of popular catchphrase around a product that was very low priced – and a little treat rather than a massive treat.'

Indeed, after complaints that ads like these were putting undue pressure on Britain's mothers, Rowntrees were asked to change their advertising slogan. After much deliberation the ad men came up with a simple solution – how about targeting fellow schoolboys instead of mothers? 'Don't forget the Fruit Gums, mum' would become 'Don't forget the Fruit Gums, *chum.*'

80 BIRDS EYE BEEFBURGERS
BEN AND MARY 1974-76

Director Alan Parker, who went on to make films such as *The Commitments,* believes he broke new ground with these ads about two burger-loving schoolkids. 'At that point in time no one was going further than London to actually cast commercials,' says Parker. 'Everybody was always middle class and handsome and everything. We thought we should take them to a different area. During that period of us desperately trying to break the middle class, beautiful teeth mould of commercials, we went to Leeds.' It was in a Leeds school that Parker and his team found Darren Cockerill and Heather McDonald, and picked them to play Ben and Mary. 'To suddenly hear a Yorkshire accent coming out of a little kid in a commercial was totally and utterly unique. It's pretty silly now when you think how normal it is. But in those days it was a complete and utter breakthrough,' Parker explains. Not everyone outside West Yorkshire was pleased with this breakthrough – Birds Eye received letters of complaint about the children's accents. Mind you, how else could they say such lines as 'Ahh, but my mam's beefburgers are a different kettle o' fish.' In fact, Cockerill and McDonald were just being natural, according to Parker. 'The kids weren't acting at all. They were just being themselves and out of that comes a naturalness and some honesty and truth, and therefore the commercials become that more believable.'

Having got used a to a good Leeds accent, the public were heartbroken when Birds Eye decided to wave goodbye to the character of Ben – dispatching him and his parents to Australia in 1976. The company was literally inundated with

letters, including over 400 signed coupons from a teen mag which ran a 'Save Ben' campaign. It was to no avail. Ben went off on a one-way trip and was replaced by twin boys who became his beloved Mary's new neighbours. Spurred on by the success of working with these children, Parker took a similar idea to the big screen and used a cast of kids to make the feature film, *Bugsy Malone.*

79 REMINGTON
VICTOR KIAM 1979

One of only a handful of American ads to make it into the Top 100, Victor Kiam's Remington Micro Shave commercials have gone down in history as naff classics. They also created a genre of bosses doin' it for themselves. 'I liked it so much I bought the company,' became a cheesy catchphrase at the end of the

Victor Kiam, President, Remington Products, Inc.

seventies. And, unlike many slogans, it was actually true. Or so Victor Kermit Kiam II would have us believe. It was missing out on one of the great clothes-fastening inventions of the twentieth century which gave Kiam the impetus to take the plunge with Remington. While Kiam was working at Playtex, a businessman contacted him to discuss a new invention – a fastening device which, he said, would supercede buttons and zips. It was called Velcro and Kiam thought it would be a huge hit. Sadly, his company declined to give the product financial backing and Mr Velcro left Kiam behind, going elsewhere to seek his fortune. Victor Kiam vowed that the next time he was offered a business deal he liked the look of he would back it with his own money. That's why he took out his chequebook in 1978.

At that point the Remington company was up for sale and although Kiam fancied the challenge, he had never tried an electric razor in his life. 'I tried it. I flipped over it. I had no idea it shaved as close as it did. Because of the product that I tried and liked so much I may have been a little enthusiastic in my attempts to buy the company. Anyway, I got the company.' All Kiam needed now was an advertising campaign to help turn the business around.

'This was before Margaret Thatcher. There was very little growth in England and very little industrialisation at the time,' he recalls. 'So I said, "Well, why don't we tell the story of how I liked the product so much I bought the company?" One of the ad agency guys came out of a deep thought process and said, "Hey, that's not a bad idea – we'll get Kevin Keegan to do it!" I said "Who's gonna believe that Kevin Keegan walked off the street and bought the company? If we're going to do it, the only person that can do it is me." We wrote a commercial there and then in about 30 seconds.'

78 OLYMPUS CAMERAS
WEDDING PHOTOGRAPHER **1977**

'David Bailey? Who's he?' was a line which came to haunt the acclaimed photographer in the late seventies. He admits that for a number of years after the ad went out he was pestered by people repeating the line to him up to ten times a day, thus making it impossible for him to take pictures in the street. Olympus is said to have been the first camera manufacturer to use TV advertising in Britain and its opening strategy was to use professional photographers to endorse their product. David Bailey, who had been a big star in the sixties but was perhaps less well known to a new generation, was considered the perfect choice to get the TV campaign going. In the first ad of the campaign Bailey is seen snapping away outside a church with a compact Olympus camera while the official wedding photographer is grappling with an over-large, old-fashioned camera. The photographer, played by actor Bryan Pringle of *The Dustbinmen* and other sitcoms fame, smugly tells Bailey he'll never shoot anything decent with a camera like that, and is bemused when Bailey tries to explain why the Olympus is a superior instrument. Pringle's assistant (played by Phil Daniels who later went on to star in the mod film *Quadrophenia*) tries to shush his boss. 'Don't you know who that is? It's David Bailey,' he says. 'David Bailey? Who's he?' replies his ignorant boss. (As well as going on to star in *Quadrophenia* Phil Daniels 'duetted' with Blur on the song *Park Life*, a tune which name-checks the famous Audi ad slogan 'Vorsprung Durch Technik').

Bailey went on to feature in a series of ads for Olympus for over 15 years, and co-starred with the likes of racing driver James Hunt, Monty Python's Eric Idle, Michael Elphick and Dawn French, who all also failed to recognise him. This despite the fact he'd been in a long-running TV commercial campaign for a number of years. Don't stars watch television? The photographer's longest-running partner was George Cole who co-starred in Olympus camera ads for four years in the late eighties.

To his credit, Patrick Lichfield *did* recognise Bailey though George Cole mistook the royal photographer for Lionel Blair. Thanks to the Bailey campaign Olympus achieved 50 per cent of the compact camera market.

77 EGGS
GO TO WORK ON AN EGG **1958**

Many people associate writer Fay Weldon with this famous campaign. But the author of novels such as *The Life And Loves of a She-Devil* is the first to admit that she didn't actually come up with the famous slogan. That honour belongs to another copywriter who Weldon was working alongside at Mather and Crowther in 1957 when a campaign was created which helped shape Weldon's outlook on life. Though many people remember Tony Hancock's involvement, the *Go To Work On An Egg* campaign went through many phases, including a period where women dressed up in high heels and short skirts as 'egg chicks' and spent breakfast time looking through housewives' dustbins for egg shells.

Half a dozen free eggs were the prize for any household whose bins included the shells, but Weldon didn't think it was the way to go about things. 'It was quite difficult to take eggs seriously,' she says. 'I remember sitting around a table with all these powerful men in suits going "Cluck, cluck, little chicken, lay a little egg for me." I would laugh – and they hated you laughing.' In fact, Weldon was one of the first women to work in television advertising and recalls how agencies really did start with a blank sheet of paper back in the mid-fifties. 'We wrote these huge, long documents. We couldn't conceive of writing anything in 15 seconds.' After much thought, the *Go To Work On An Egg* idea was dreamt up.

'The campaign was fun. It was very wholesome and was meant to keep women in their place.' In the mid-sixties the ad agency decided comedy star Hancock was the man to take the campaign forward. Fay Weldon had reservations. 'He was terribly unhappy. Advertising was considered really very vulgar and rather low and if you were reduced to doing it – especially for an actor or a well-known person – it was seen as something of a disgrace and he [Hancock] certainly felt as such. And I just felt terribly sorry somehow asking him to do it.' Despite his discomfort at being involved, Hancock went on to make over a dozen commercials for the Egg Marketing Board, usually accompanied by actress Patricia Hayes.

The campaign was a boost for egg sales, but Hancock remained unhappy. He committed suicide in Australia in 1968.

76 BRITISH RAIL
RELAX 1989

Tony Kaye is one of modern advertising's more colourful characters – a former messenger boy and loo cleaner who failed to get into art college. When this commercial was offered to him, Kaye was in need of a change of fortunes. 'I'd only been involved in the making of two television commercials. People said I'd never achieve any success. At one point I was on the platform at Piccadilly Circus and looking at the line and considering throwing myself on it.'

In an effort to get work, Kaye pulled a series of bizarre stunts, including 'throwing things off buildings' and 'running into ad agencies and kidnapping people'. It was, Kaye recalls, all to no avail: 'I didn't get any work so I went to the cinema for five years and watched six movies a day.' Although this stood his creativity in good stead it didn't pay the rent, so Kaye was relieved when he got a phone call from Saatchi and Saatchi, asking him to make a commercial for British Rail. 'They must have thought, "If I give it to this bloke he is going to work on it night and day",' says Kaye.

BR wanted something new and Saatchi and Saatchi believed Tony Kaye's vision could provide it. 'I shot a hundred thousand feet of film. I had no idea what I was doing...No, I *did* know what I was doing; I was making sure this was going to be a fantastic, successful thing – and, thank God, it was.' Forget Jimmy Savile opening his briefcase on the train while drinking BR coffee; Kaye went for mood instead of realism and delivered one of the most talked-about ads of the eighties. The ad, shown in sepia, showed ordinary (but interesting) people relaxing while a Leon Redbone track chugged along in the background. It turned the BR experience into something out of the movies – and not the reality of late trains and no seats. In fact, although the ad industry loved Kaye's work, not all members of the public were impressed. British Rail had to deal with letters from passengers who felt the ad bore no resemblance to real life.

Tony Kaye went on to direct many more groundbreaking ads before moving to the US to become a film director.

75 MARS
A MARS A DAY **1958**

Mars was one of the first chocolate bars to be featured in a British TV commercial, making its debut in the fifties with a *Stars Love Mars* campaign with Bob Monkhouse and Petula Clark. In 1959 ad agency Masius and Ferguson came up with the surely scientifically unprovable slogan: 'A Mars a day helps you work, rest and play' – the work of a young ad man called Murray Walker, who went on to become

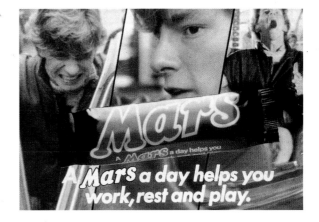

TV's voice of Formula One racing. Although most people remember the 'Mars a day' slogan because of its jingle, the ad campaign survived without any musical accompaniment for 14 years. In the fifties and sixties many Mars-eating characters, from window cleaners to 'dolly bird' disco girls, were all seen enjoying the benefits of chewy milk chocolate. A Mars bar was even compared to the ceremonial Changing of the Guards – 'Part of our way of life,' ran the commentary.

It wasn't until 1973 that the all-familiar jingle came in – usually after the bit where the viewers are lectured for ten seconds on the wonders of glucose. Much-parodied for its claim – can a Mars bar *really* make you work, rest and play? – the famous slogan was finally dropped in 1997 because it wasn't deemed 'sexy' enough. 'We want to show energy, both physically and emotionally,' said a Mars spokesman at the time, introducing a new ad featuring a dying American Indian rejuvenated by a Mars bar. 'It's a taste for life', became the new slogan. Two years later it was all change again and Mars went into the new millennium with the strapline 'Every day should be this good'. Neither were a patch on the original, which must go down as one of the classic ad slogans of the last 50 years. ' "A Mars A Day Helps You Work Rest and Play" has become common parlance – partly through repetition and partly because it summed up everything they used to say in their advertising,' says Rupert Howell, president of the Institute of Practitioners in Advertising.

'Is it true? Well, it's hard to say. I mean, they've certainly been allowed to maintain the line under intense scrutiny from various authorities and watchdogs because the product *is* an energy-giving product.'

74 LEGO
KIPPER **1980**

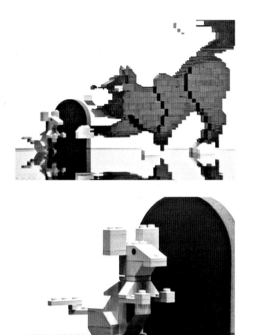

In the seventies, ads for toys usually showed kids getting dizzy with excitement over an action doll or Scalextric, while mum looked on. But *this* ad, made by TBWA, was different. There were no kids and there were no mums. And it worked on two levels. Not only did kids enjoy it but mums and dads thought it was pretty cool too. The ad showed a series of shapes that could be built with Lego (Latin for 'I am joining together' and Danish for 'Play well'). 'You see, I was standing outside my mouse-hole the other day when all of a sudden comes this cat,' (says the announcer, as we see a Lego cat and mouse). 'So quick as a flash I turned into a Lego dog...but the cat turned into a dragon...so I turned into a fire engine.'

Over the course of the ad the viewers see a mouse, a cat, a dog, a dragon, a fire engine, a submarine, a submarine-eating kipper, an anti-kipper ballistic missile, a missile cruncher and an elephant...who's scared off by the mouse from the start of the ad. The commercial was an immediate hit and at one point appeared in the *Guinness Book of Records* as the ad with the most awards to its name. However, the commercial only ran on British TV for a few months before being replaced by something more conventional with kids and mums.

As for the voice-over, the agency thought about comedian and kids' presenter Mike Reid before plumping for Tommy Cooper whose voice went down well in research. Even foreigners who didn't know Cooper found it funny. Unfortunately, Cooper was ill when the time came to record. An impressionist had to step in. It didn't matter; everyone thought it was Tommy Cooper anyway.

73 MURRAY MINTS
TOO GOOD TO HURRY MINTS 1955

The first animated Murray Mints ad, with marching soldiers in bearskin hats, has the distinction of being the first TV commercial to be voted 'ad of the year' in Britain.

One of 1955's more inventive ads, it was chosen by broadcaster Alistair Cooke, of BBC Radio's *Letter From America* fame, to show the Americans how the British could make world-beating TV commercials. It was also one of the first British ads to have a jingle that was soon being hummed in factories, pubs and offices all over the country – popular enough to be released as a single by Decca Records in 1957. The ad was created by artists John Halas and Joy Batchelor, who a few months earlier had made a critically acclaimed animated version of George Orwell's *Animal Farm*. The now famous jingle was written by Harold Fields and Joe Roncoroni (who wrote the music) and Harold 'Boogie' Barnes, who wrote the lyrics:

'Murray Mints, Murray Mints, too good to hurry mints.
Why make haste when you can taste the hint of mint in Murray Mints?'

Composer Cliff Adams had already had success with his band The Stargazers before the birth of ITV, but when the ad agency rang him in August 1955, a new career path was opening up. 'I knew nothing about advertising at all but the chap asked if we could sing a jingle they had for Murray Mints,' says Adams. 'Anyway, we did it and it seemed to catch on. I then saw for the first time the power of commercial television. I started to take a very keen interest in it and very soon started composing and writing, as well as performing music for commercials.' At the end of 1955, the Murray Mints ad topped the poll, beating Shell and Guinness into second and third place, when the *News Chronicle* asked readers to nominate their favourite commercials in the first year of ITV.

72 FAIRY LIQUID
HANDS THAT DO DISHES 1961

Cliff Adams was one of two British jingle writers who seemed to have the entire advertising jingle industry sewn up in the sixties and seventies – the other was Johnny Johnson. Like Adams, Johnson started off in light entertainment on BBC radio and was the leader of a vocal group. Johnson was involved in the ad industry from the very start, being collared by an ad company in 1954, but it wasn't until the

early sixties that he struck gold, when he was asked to write a jingle for a Fairy Liquid campaign. This showed mum at the kitchen sink and adoring daughter playing nearby. 'Now hands that do dishes can be soft as your face, with Mild Green Fairy Liquid' was a soaring melody once heard never forgotten.

But back in 1961, when the advertising campaign began, washing-up liquid was still a new product. At that point only one in five British households used washing-up liquid, as opposed to powders or soap. By the end of its first year of advertising, six out of ten households were using Fairy Liquid. That's the power of TV advertising. Many celebrities have been involved in Fairy Liquid campaigns over the years, but most people recall Nanette Newman as the public face of the product. Born in 1939, Newman was the star of TV and films like *International Velvet* and *The Stepford Wives* before starring in the campaign.

By 1993 a poll linking celebrities with products showed that Newman and Fairy Liquid went lovely soft hand-in-hand. Over 60 per cent of people questioned associated her with Fairy Liquid, well ahead of the second place ad featuring ever-present George Cole, this time in a Leeds Permanent Building Society campaign. Nanette Newman's successful involvement with Fairy Liquid ran for 12 years, until the product was brought into the nineties with a new image. No longer was the sight of a middle-class woman washing thousands of dirty dishes with one bottle an attractive advertising proposition; the new campaign showed blokes doing the washing-up after cooking for their girlfriends. The original ad, showing a young girl asking 'Mummy, why are your hands so soft?', back in 1965 provided one of the first TV roles for actress and child model Leslie Ash (pictured above).

71 THE GUARDIAN
POINTS OF VIEW 1986

Many of our greatest ads have ended up as television moments which initiated great debate. But this is the only entry in the chart that ended up being used in an assault trial at the Old Bailey. 'We got lots of phone calls from people wanting the ad for various reasons – usually colleges and universities,' recalls its creator, John Webster. 'But the most interesting was from a chap who was up for trial. He wanted a copy to use in his defence.

Unfortunately, we never heard whether he got off or not.' It was one of the most thought-provoking 30 seconds British advertising has ever produced. And to think that it was all shot in Southwark in a day.

In the commercial we see a skinhead running along the pavement in pursuit of a businessman. The camera cuts to a different angle and we see the youth seemingly trying to wrestle the man's briefcase out of his hands. Cut to a third angle and we realise the skinhead's real intentions – pushing the businessman out of the way of a shower of bricks falling from an overhead. The voice-over finishes by stating: 'It's only when you get the whole picture that you can fully understand what's going on.' Says Webster: 'At the time most newspapers had proprietors who were dictating the policy of the papers. The *Guardian* prided itself in not having a strong proprietor, giving writers the space to write their own viewpoint.'

The grainy, black and white documentary feel of the commercial was inspired by a photo of British troops running down a street in Northern Ireland. No music was needed and a simple voice-over sufficed. Director Paul Weiland was brought in to shoot an ad he still calls 'a gift...and probably the most intelligent commercial I've ever been involved in'. The plan was to shoot the ad all in one take from three different cameras filming simultaneously, but Weiland had a problem. 'I couldn't get the shots right because every time I got a good shot and I set the next camera up the first camera was always in shot.' He ended up shooting the ad over several takes from three different angles. 'The commercial turned out pretty good though,' he says. Some might think that an understatement.

Four years after the ad was made, Weiland was voted Britain's 'Commercial Director of the Decade'. In February 2000, the *Guardian* ad was voted 'Greatest Ad Ever' by some of the country's leading ad makers of the last 40 years.

70 CRESTA
FROTHY MAN 1972

From ads about open-minded broadsheets to spots promoting soft drinks...*admeister* John Webster set his mind to all sorts of tasks in the seventies and eighties – and usually came out of each campaign with a couple of awards to his name. A photo of the 'Troubles' had been the inspiration for the look of the *Guardian* ad; it was Webster's love of the movies that provided the spur for this adventure in advertising animation. 'We were trying to think of a way of selling this soft drink and selling appetite appeal,' he recalls. 'I went to see *Easy Rider,* which was a big hit at the time. There's a wonderful scene in it where Jack Nicholson's character comes out of prison and takes his first drink of whisky for a week, taking it from a small bottle in his pocket. He does this lovely *nick, nick, nick* sort of spasm of appreciation. It was brilliant. I thought "That's great. The kids will love this." We devised our own version of that.' Cresta was originally sold as a health drink for adults, but its owners decided it should be re-marketed for children. Webster went home from the pictures and began playing around with words – Cresta, cresta run, snow, polar bears. He'd seen another film called *Taking Off* about a teenage girl running away to a distant land with a hippy boyfriend and wondered what it would be like if the Cresta bear ran away from the North Pole because he loved the drink so much.

Webster had soon created a line-drawing figure brought to life in 15 ads by the remarkably named Canadian actor Thick Wilson who also voiced the Honey Monster. Singing songs like Elvis Presley's *Teddy Bear*, complete with backing vocalists, the groovy, laid-back bear with the catchphrase 'It's frothy, man' was an instant hit among Britain's youth – especially with its Nicholsonesque facial contortions. Says Webster: 'Every time our hero Cresta bear drank he went into this ridiculous routine spasm that all the kids were trying to copy in the playground. Each year of the advertising campaign we changed the spasm to a new set of noises. The kids were with us – they changed in the playground! It was kind of cool for them if they could do it. It makes me feel old now because I interview people for jobs and two or three of them have remembered the Cresta ads and could quote the scripts verbatim and even remember the spasm!'

69 DUNLOP
TESTED FOR THE UNEXPECTED 1993

'I see ads like this as a creative sacrifice – so that other, better films will get made elsewhere.' So says Trevor Beattie, one of the admen of the nineties, thanks to his work on campaigns like 'Fcuk' for French Connection and Wonderbra's 'Hello Boys' posters. Beattie is talking about a controversial ad which might not have shifted *that* many tyres for Dunlop but was a bold and very different commercial that influenced a new generation of ad makers.

Set with the task of creating an ad to demonstrate the reliability of Dunlop tyres, ad writer Tom Carty and his creative partner Walter Campbell set out to show 'the most amazing demonstration'. 'We thought of the old cliché – you are driving along and a kid steps out in front of you, and that's the time when you really need your tyres,' explains Carty. 'We thought – take that kind of cliché and put it into a completely different context and landscape.' Carty and Campbell came up with a surreal environment ruled by a fat, bald character intent on causing drivers unexpected problems, like gigantic marbles on the road and grand pianos falling out of the sky.

It was still a battle of good against evil, and the agency believed only one man could make the battle plan work. Tony Kaye had made the British Rail ad three years earlier and was by then in America making ads on a grander scale. With Kaye in creative control *Tested For The Unexpected* was a £500,000 shoot, filmed near Los Angeles. He used ten different cameras shooting simultaneously to capture the action – complete with body- and-face-painted characters, orange skies and purple trees (though the ad was shot in black and white and colourised for effect in post-production). When the commercial was aired (set to the equally nightmarish soundtrack of the Velvet Underground's *Venus In Furs*) the response was immediate – and divided. One critic was to call it 'the most surreal, abstract bit of impressionism ever produced by a major agency'.

68 BRITISH GAS
IF YOU SEE SID **1986**

Perhaps Margaret Thatcher was among the voters for this ad. The 'If you see Sid, tell him' campaign, encouraging the public to buy shares in British Gas, couldn't have happened without her privatisation policies of the mid-eighties. In the year 2000, share ownership among the general public might not seem such a big deal. But back in 1986 ad agencies had to think of a way of promoting what was still seen as 'a really strange notion' according to one man who had to come up with ideas for the British Gas campaign. After weeks of coffee drinking and deliberating, Rupert Howell and his colleagues at Young and Rubicam eventually came up with a concept. 'One of the things that happens when there's a great piece of gossip is that people pass it on to each other in all sorts of bizarre places,' says Howell.

'So the strategy was to have this sort of mythical figure who we were all seeking to tell about British Gas privatisation; it was just an observation on how news travels amongst the population.' As for the origins of 'Sid', Howell explains that the name was picked because it was 'short and a great name...and I suppose we were referring to people like Sid James'. The idea went down well with then Energy Minister Peter Walker, to whom Howell had to present the idea for the campaign. By a bizarre coincidence, says Howell, the minister had a brother called Sid who lived on a hilltop in Wales. He gave the campaign his immediate blessing.

After a series of ads set in rural settings such as the Scottish isles, and featuring 'ordinary people' like nurses and fishermen, the campaign did catch up with the mysterious Sid. The location was a misty clifftop in Wales, but due to the heavy mist, his identity would rather cleverly be kept secret forever. The slogan 'If you see Sid, tell him' entered the popular vocabulary – 'Sids' became a media term for small shareholders – and the campaign was a tremendous success. Eight million people registered for British Gas shares, four million buying them.

67 SONY
ARMCHAIR **1995**

There's something about Sony and armchairs. In the space of ten years Sony came up with two ads featuring the comfy chair. Both were made by the same British ad agency – Boase Massimi Pollitt. Apart from the chairs, the ads couldn't have been more different. The Sony armchair ad which *didn't* make it into the chart was a static shot showing the phases of a man's life – from baby to

grandfather. If that ad was brilliant in its simplicity, *this* Sony ad was both complex and dangerous. It featured a be-suited man free-falling through the sky in an armchair, hurtling towards the earth at great speed. Just as he is about to hit the ground the armchair/skydiver changes the channel on his TV – and instantly finds himself safe and sound back in his front room. Finally, his cat falls from the ceiling into his lap. The message was clear – watching the latest Sony television with 'surround-sound' was one hell of a moving experience. Daniel Barber, who shot the ad, was the only director the ad agency approached to consider doing the shoot for real – everyone else suggested shooting it with a static armchair in a studio with images of the sky projected behind.

Not surprisingly, Barber's way was more complex. Both stunt man and cameraman (Tom Saunders, who shot the film *Point Break*) had to fall through the sky in hot pursuit. The jump was performed nearly 20 times and before each jump the stunt man shook hands with each member of the crew – in case he never saw them again. The man in the chair at the end of the ad is the same man falling through the sky at 150mph. One of the most difficult jobs for the team was finding a location where armchairs could hit the ground without wiping out the locals, or their cattle. Eventually, the ad makers settled on a huge ranch just outside Los Angeles, where *Little House on the Prairie* had been shot. The ranch owner had one condition – if armchairs, actors or cameramen hit his cattle the production team would have to compensate him. Fortunately, no actors or cattle were hurt during the making of this £500,000 commercial. But 33 armchairs did come to grief after being tossed out of a helicopter at 12,000ft. Two were never found.

66 TOSHIBA
'ULLO TOSH 1984

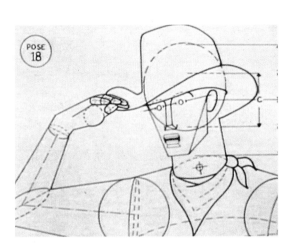

In the early eighties a then-unknown comedy actor called Alexei Sayle played the part of a mad landlord in the anarchic BBC comedy show *The Young Ones*. In one episode Sayle burst into a song called *'Ullo John Got A New Motor?'* The song was subsequently released as a single and reached Number Eight in the British charts. A short while later the TV manufacturer Toshiba was searching for a campaign to make their TVs stand out from those of other Japanese companies. They felt that one of the major factors influencing the purchase of a TV set was the make – and that Toshiba simply wasn't well known enough as a brand. The idea the ad agency came up with was to give their campaign a distinctly *British* feel. They slowed down Alexei Sayle's song, changed the title to *'Ullo Tosh, Got A Toshiba?'* ('Tosh' was a term of endearment that uncles called nephews in parts of London) and brought in Ian Dury to sing it. Suddenly, Toshiba seemed more East End than Far East. Perhaps this wasn't surprising as the ad writer was Dave Trott, who had come up with the idea for Courage Best's *Gertcha* ad featuring the Cockney duo Chas 'n' Dave. The Toshiba ad used a 50-year-old animation technique called *rotascoping* (first seen in Disney's *Snow White*) to show a robot-type 'Blueprint Man' extolling the virtues of Toshiba's latest TV sets.

It worked. Before the campaign there was a 2 per cent awareness of Toshiba products. Six weeks later the figure had rocketed to 30 per cent and sales rose by 45 per cent.

65 BIRDS EYE FISH FINGERS
CAPT BIRDS EYE **1968**

In 1998 the world saw a new Captain Birds Eye. He was a 6ft model with film star looks, stubble and a chisel jaw – more Indiana Jones than Gilbert and Sullivan and not an 'Ahoy!' or an 'A-ha!' to be heard. Thus, over 30 years the good captain had been transformed from a friendly 'unc' to a gorgeous hunk. The original captain, introduced in 1968, was played by London-born actor John Hewer. It was not his first commercial for Birds Eye; in the early sixties Hewer had 'popped' up in the peas commercial which went 'sweet as the moment when the pod went pop'. More appropriately, he had also been a navigator in the Navy and a sales conference director for Birds Eye.

The Captain Birds Eye campaign was a marked change in advertising for the frozen food company. Up until then it had been commissioning ads that highlighted the practicality of cooking its products. 'Children love fish fingers. There are no bones and they're already cooked and crumbled,' said the announcer. With Captain Birds Eye they were appealing directly to the kids. 'Captain Birds Eye owes a great deal to Robert Newton as Long John Silver, and probably to Tony Hancock impersonating Robert Newton doing Long John Silver,' says Barry Day, who co-created a campaign to appeal to the mums as well as the kids.

John Hewer, these days in his late seventies and living in London, recalls the audition for Captain Birds Eye: 'They chose about 20 of us and sent us down to the Cutty Sark at Greenwich. They stuck a beard on me, sent me to the edge of the gangway and made me say "Ahoy!" and "A ha!" and rubbish like that.'

In 1971, after a long and successful run, Birds Eye temporarily disposed of Hewer – *The Times* ran a mock obituary stating that the captain had been lost at sea – and replaced him with another character and actor. But Captain Birds Eye was brought back by popular demand – and in glorious technicolour – three years later, surviving until 1998.

64 SCHWEPPES
SHH...YOU KNOW WHO **1963**

"Say when..."

William Franklyn was playing a secret agent in the ITV series *Top Secret* when he was approached to take a similar part in a TV campaign for Schweppes Tonic Water. It was the early sixties, and spy yarns like James Bond and *The Avengers* were very much part of the popular culture of the time. The Schweppes ad took the theme into the ad breaks, though this time it was the name of the company that Franklyn was trying to keep top secret, helped by the teasing catchphrase 'Tonic water from...shhh...you know who'. The ads featured Franklyn keeping his cool in a variety of situations. One of the earliest showed him talking tonic water while an entire building is destroyed around him.

The Australian-born actor remembers how easy it was to film an ad campaign in those days: 'We were left alone to get on and shoot commercials for eight or nine years. Someone from the office would phone and say "Can we come down and see you fellows?" We said, "We'd love to see somebody – we never see anybody!" There were no focus groups. They just found that the commercials we made seemed to work.' One of the most famous Schweppes ads saw Franklyn pouring an inferior tonic water into a parrot's drinking dish at a party. The parrot drinks it, does a somersault and drops off its perch. The ad was taken around the world by agency Ogilvy Mather as an example of the elite in British TV advertising. It was all good fun for Franklyn and his colleagues. 'We were very serious about what we were doing but we never took ourselves seriously. My mother was sitting in a theatre once when I was doing a play in London and a woman behind her said: "Oh, this is the man who does the Schweppes show." You see, it was a show in that you had an entertainment of 30 seconds which happened to be selling a product at the same time.'

Franklyn was following in the footsteps of Benny Hill, who played a West Country publican in early sixties commercials for Schweppes. Before that, the company's managing director had done the job himself. Fortunately, copies of the Franklyn Schweppes ads have been kept for posterity so we can see the sort of character that made him a household name in *Top Secret*. It's just as well; sadly the entire *Top Secret* archive was wiped to save videotape in the early sixties.

63 YORKIE
COAST TO COAST 1976

In the mid-seventies, long-distance lorry drivers became hip. Instead of being seen as tattooed former squaddies cutting up motorists and wolf-whistling at anything in a skirt, the British truck driver became an unlikely working class hero. CB radio was a popular hobby, pop songs celebrating truckers made it onto *Top of the Pops,* and Rowntrees used the long-distance lorry driver to sell the most manly bar of chocolate ever made. 'I pounded the road from coast to coast, Yorkie and me holding on,' went the country and western-style theme tune, as we saw the amiable truck driver going

about his business, crossing the Humber Bridge accompanied by his trusty chocolate bar. The ad campaign was all about making chocolate – traditionally a female product – into something Britain's manliest men would be proudly seen with. Cultural historian Robert Hewison believes there's plenty of sub-text in the famous campaign. 'They made it "a man's thing" by making it very like a man's "thing". The ad starts off with a phallic-shaped bridge and then you have the lorry, this big powerful male object, powering through the traffic. When he eats the chocolate he doesn't eat it as a woman might; he chews it off as though he were a prehistoric male tearing flesh off a stegosaurus bone.'

At the end of the commercial, having exchanged glances with a pretty girl in an open-top car, our hero is seen placing the remainder of his Yorkie in his top pocket 'as if it were his cigarettes, a pipe or, of course, a condom,' comments Hewison. Broadcaster Stuart Maconie believes the ad could only have worked in the mid-seventies. 'What looks antiquated about the Yorkie campaign now is this concept of the lorry driver as a cheery knight of the road, chewing on his chocolate bar instead of high cholesterol bacon and eggs at 4 o'clock in the morning in Charnock Richard Service Station,' says Maconie. 'There's no road rage, he's looking very calm and obviously his lorry's full of Yorkies rather than an entire family of Romanian gypsies that he's bringing over to avoid their terrible political system.' Despite the reality gap the ad *was* a tremendous success.

62 BRITISH AIRWAYS
FACE 1989

Sometimes an ad can turn the fortunes of a company around. Hugh Hudson's commercial for British Airways is one such ad. Before this literally gave the company a 'human face' BA had gone through a period of losing £100 million a year. By 1993 the company was reported to be the world's most successful airline. Hudson, whose directing credits include *Chariots of Fire* and *Greystoke,* produced the ad at a cost of over £1 million. It had a cast of 4,000, and was seen by over 600 million people in 70 countries. It was truly a global project, making Coca Cola's *Teach The World To Sing* campaign look like a home movie, and yet Hudson calls it 'the easiest, most relaxed commercial I've ever made'. The idea was to show the eyes, ears, nose and mouth of an enormous face coming together, all seen from a bird's-eye-view over Utah. The link was that British Airways claimed to bring 24 million people together every year. Each part of the face was played by American high school students, who were brought by bus to the desert locations.

The students were dressed in different colours to collectively form a face. It was a job which needed the incredible choreographing skills of American Judy Chaboia, as Hudson explains: 'We had a fantastic organiser for moving people around. Judy had done the crowd movements at the Olympic Games. She was like a dancer, rehearsing each group of people.' While the painstaking organisation was going on at ground level, Hudson spent most of the shoot in a helicopter with the camera crew. 'Strangely, it wasn't that difficult to film. It was all in the preparation. But it was a long shoot – three weeks or something – very long, very expensive. The people putting up the money, British Airways, had to have enormous faith that we were going to achieve something and not just make a mess. The credit goes to the school kids, all from local schools, who were able to make a face, form an eye, wink and form the Earth. All we did was sit in a helicopter till they got it right.'

61 MAXELL
ISRAELITES 1990

One of the funniest ads of the past decade was inspired by one of the dourest of rock music icons.

In 1965 Bob Dylan made a promotional film for his song *Subterranean Homesick Blues.* He was seen standing in front of the camera holding the lyrics of his song on a series of cue cards. Once one set of words had passed, Dylan threw the card down and showed the next. Twenty-five years later ad agency Howell Henry Chaldecott Lury took the idea, married it with Desmond Dekker's reggae hit *Israelites,* and produced a modern classic based on our tendency to mishear pop lyrics. Actor Larrington Walker played the part of the dude in the knit cap with the off-the-wall translation. The cue cards bore the lyrics:

'Get up in the morning
Sleeping for bread, sir,
Sold out to every monk
And beefhead.
Oh oh, me ears are alight.
Why find my kids?
They buck up and a-leave me.
Darling Cheese Head
I was yards too greasy
Oh oh, my ears are alight.'

As the song fades away, Walker's final cards read: 'I think that's what he says, but I need to hear it on a Maxell.' The ad was a welcome break from other commercials for high-performance audio cassettes which tried to impress with a sales pitch.

In ads for a youth-orientated product usually associated with taping pop music, humour wasn't often considered – which was why this Maxell ad stood out, picking up a string of awards. In fact, the *Israelites* spot was so popular that Maxell followed it up with similarly misheard lyrics from The Skids' New Wave hit *Into The Valley.* The amount spent on both ads might have been small but often the simplest ideas are the best. The campaign promptly pushed Maxell from fifth to second place in its market.

6o RICE KRISPIES
SNAP, CRACKLE AND POP **1955**

The 'Snap, Crackle and Pop' characters must be about the oldest in British TV advertising, having first been seen on a Kellogg's packet back in 1928. Rice Krispies were first introduced in the United States in the year before the Great Depression. But it was another ten years before the cereal that makes those weird noises when you pour milk on it was made in the UK, at a factory in Manchester. The agency J Walter Thompson was then brought in to handle the advertising. Due to a shortage of rice, the cereal was withdrawn from British breakfast tables during the Second World War, but it returned to our kitchens in 1951. The three animated characters first appeared on British TV screens in the late fifties, dancing around the breakfast table like hi-energy elves, singing: 'It's snap, crackle and pop, so rise and shine, Rice Krispies time.'

The ad agency took a new approach (and some might say a bit of a risk) in the early sixties when their cartoon characters were replaced by an ad featuring the sounds of The Rolling Stones. Mick Jagger and his pals failed miserably to live up to the headline, 'Would you let your daughter marry a Rolling Stone?' by singing a harmless ditty about the virtues of snap, crackle and pop. Another famous personality made his acting debut in a Rice Krispies ad in the seventies. Jonathan Ross was a slip of a lad when he cycled home from school and munched on some Rice Krispies at the breakfast table. However, despite these temporary impositions from showbiz stars, Kelloggs' cartoon characters have lived on into the 21st century in the latest series of ads – snapping, crackling and popping as loudly as ever.

59 AUDI
VORSPRUNG DURCH TECHNIK 1984

There has always been a reluctance in the UK to buying foreign cars – and, for some, especially cars made by the Germans. Audi tackled this issue directly in a campaign that actually promoted the car's Germanic qualities – a tactic that could easily have gone horribly wrong, according to psychologist Dr David Lewis. 'Audi was taking something of a risk by emphasising the Germanic nature of their cars,' he says. 'Had they made the advertisements five or ten years earlier they would have aroused

anger and hysteria in the media.' Despite the fact that, traditionally, Germans on primetime British TV were either mocked (*Fawlty Towers)* or seen as the enemy (*Dad's Army)*, ad creators John Hegarty and Barbara Noakes were given the brief of sticking a flag in the car to make it state: 'I am German.' Hegarty first spotted the phrase 'Vorsprung Durch Technik' on a poster in a German Audi factory. Asked what it meant, a German worker told him 'You haven't really got a word for it, but sort of "moving ahead with technology".'

The slogan stuck with Hegarty. When he got back to England and started looking for a common factor to bring together a TV, poster and print campaign, he remembered what he had seen in the factory. The phrase '...as they say in Germany' was added, and a memorable slogan was born. Public response was negative when the idea was researched, but Audi and agency Bartle Bogle Hegarty went with their gut instinct and ran the campaign. Though the style of the ads changed over the years the tag line (voiced by *Butterflies* actor Geoffrey Palmer) linked them all. One of the most memorable ads of the campaign, showing a family by a swimming pool, managed to both praise German technology and allude to a British stereotype of them. The message was clear – invest in an Audi 'if you want to be on the beach before the Germans'. Dr David Lewis believes he knows why the campaign boosted Audi sales. 'It plugged into a stereotypic view we have about the Germans, namely that they may have no sense of humour but they do know how to produce very well-engineered cars.'

58 HOFMEISTER
FOLLOW THE BEAR 1983

Hofmeister had already used a bear to promote their beer before this campaign, but the ad agency BMP considered that incarnation too frightening for television. Instead, they had to give the bear an image makeover. 'I got the inspiration from the Fonz in *Happy Days*,' recalls John Webster. 'He used to walk around like he was Mr Cool, so we turned the bear into an English version of The Fonz. We gave him sharp clothes and dreamt up the line "Follow The Bear".'

The idea was to create an ad that would get talked about down the pub – an ad that was cool and funny and presented the right image. George, the now-friendly Hofmeister bear with a swaggering walk, hit the spot. He was played by a 4ft 6in Hungarian strongman called Ivan who performed in circuses and clubs. 'He had this wonderful, swaggering walk which was perfect for us,' says Webster. 'We put him inside the bear suit and the walk you see is *his* walk – he'd walk like that quite naturally.'

George was always pictured as the cool guy turning tricks on the dance floor

and even coming out on top on the Sunday football field. And wherever he went, he was accompanied by two blokes – because in traditional beer ads the heroes always drank in numbers. As Webster explains: 'You never had a guy on his own, drinking. That would make him a loner and against the rules for a beer ad. And you never had just two men drinking together – because people would then think they were gay. It was always three – never one, or two – always three.' But just when things were going well, disaster struck. Lager louts started to hit the national headlines, smashing up trains and causing bother in rural pubs – the drinking holes of the Tory voter. 'The Government had to be seen to be doing something – so they took off George,' recalls Webster. 'He was banned because he incited these lager louts, apparently.' George was temporarily replaced by a hedgehog who had the same swaggering walk, but somehow 'Follow The Hedgehog' just didn't feel the same. The Hofmeister hedgehog was spiked.

57 AFTER EIGHTS
DINNER PARTY **1963**

Actors have been gathering around the most sophisticated dinner tables in British TV advertising for nearly 40 years now. These days, computer technology can unite the likes of Marilyn Monroe, Stephen Fry and Elizabeth Hurley, all of them sharing the After Eights and after-dinner conversation. But in the early days the ads weren't full of stars – just bow-tied and ball-gowned couples exchanging knowing glances as well as the chocolate mints. The product (and television campaign) was launched in 1963 when children weren't supposed to be awake after early evening, the name 'After Eight' being adopted to suggest something rather sophisticated and adult for the grown-up members of the household.

After Eights ads in the sixties might have shown the aristocracy with their dress cutlery, butlers and silver mint holders, but that probably wasn't who the campaign was aimed at. 'The dinner party ads were not aimed at the kind of people who were in the ads, because that kind of people wouldn't be seen dead serving After Eights dinner mints,' suggests Rupert Howell, president of the Institute of Practitioners in Advertising. 'But it was a classic case of playing to old British class values and the sort of aspirations of the middle classes to be seen as a bit more upper class – and it did so in such a wonderfully clever way.

'You just know that every dinner table in Surbiton had a box of After Eights on it after that...but none of them did at Whatknot Hall in Staffordshire or wherever the ad might have been shot.'

5 6 FIAT
HANDBUILT BY ROBOTS 1979

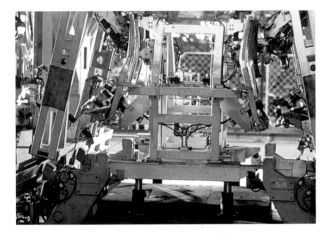

One evening in 1979, television viewers who hadn't gone to the loo in the middle of *News at Ten* saw something very unusual – a commercial break completely taken up by one ad. It was a two-minute triumph showing a car being put together in a factory – and not a dirty blue overall in sight. The original idea for an ad to promote the new Italian car was to use smoke coming out of the Vatican as a sign that a new car had been born. But the ad makers eventually decided it too controversial. Back at the drawing board, writer Paul Weiland remembered an item he had seen on the TV show *Tomorrow's World* about the Fiat factory in Italy where cars were put together by robots. He tracked the footage down and decided it could form the basis of the new Fiat campaign. 'In Europe the car was called the "Ritmo" so I thought "What kind of music can I put with this?"' recalls Weiland. 'My knowledge of classical music was zilch but I remembered something called Figaro and thought "Figaro sounds like Ritmo!" I put this music to it and everyone thought it was great.' If that part was easy, the filming of the commercial turned out to be a nightmare.

When the production team got to the Fiat plant in Turin they found themselves in the middle of a tense situation. 'When we arrived there, there was a strike, and we got locked in to the factory,' recalls director Hugh Hudson. 'We were locked in so we could make the commercial and since the film is about robots there was nobody operating – just someone to press the button. All the workers were out but we were in making the film.' 'The commercial was quite expensive at that time (around £300,000),' adds Paul Weiland. 'But they probably lost about seven million in production, because every two seconds we were having to stop the machines!'

The finished ad had no voice-over and ended on a simple caption 'Handbuilt by Robots'. Many ad makers believe its intelligent combination of music and camerawork make it one of the best TV commercials ever shown in this country.

55 WHISKAS
EIGHT OUT OF TEN CATS 1976

And yet, more people voted for a series of cheap ads showing middle-aged cat owners in their kitchens in the seventies and eighties. Members of the public, like Mrs Betty Davies from Tolworth, were pictured in their kitchenettes dishing out the moist and meaty Whiskas Supermeat for their beloved moggie, whilst explaining how much Tiddles did indeed love the brand. 'If he could speak I think Whiskas Supermeat would be his first words,' claimed Mrs Davies, in a statement for which the words 'hypothetical situation' were invented. But the voiced-over claim at the end of the early ads – 'Eight out of ten owners said their cats preferred it' – failed to convince broadcaster Stuart Maconie. 'Whiskas was sold with the bold claim that eight out of ten cats preferred it – which was clearly not true,' he says. 'For instance, how can you tell what your cat prefers? Has it written

you a note? Cats, I would have thought, are pretty keen on food generally.' Someone somewhere must have agreed because, in the eighties, the tag line was changed to 'Eight out of ten owners *who expressed a preference* said their cats preferred it'...which, if you think about it, doesn't make much sense either.

Whiskas ads went from the sublime to the ridiculous when, in the late nineties, they unveiled the world's first TV advert for cats. The ad cost £750,000 to produce, and Whiskas confidently predicted that 60 per cent of cats 'might' react to the pet-friendly advert which showed lots of bright lights, sudden movements and toy canaries bouncing up and down on bits of elastic. But how did they know for sure that the other 40 per cent definitely wouldn't react? Come back Mrs Betty Davies and your talking cat. All is forgiven.

54 HOLSTEN PILS
GRIFF RHYS JONES **1983**

The makers of Holsten Pils have looked to a variety of personalities, from Donald Pleasance to characters from *The Fast Show*, to promote their lager, but none have been quite as memorable as the comedian Griff Rhys Jones.

The American actor Steve Martin made a film in 1982 called *Dead Men Don't Wear Plaid*. In it, his character interacts with people cut out of classic Hollywood films of the thirties and forties. It was a clever trick, and when Axel Chaldicott and Steve Henry of ad agency Gold Greenlees Trott saw it they immediately thought it

was a great idea for an ad. Chaldicott and Henry were working on a brief for Holsten Pils lager and soon found that the two could be combined brilliantly. All they needed now was a British Steve Martin to carry it off.

Griff Rhys Jones had risen to television fame in the comedy show *Not The Nine O'Clock News* and would prove the perfect choice. Over the next seven years Rhys Jones had the chance to 'work' with Marilyn Monroe, John Wayne and Humphrey Bogart – all long dead, but eerily brought back to life with the skill of Rhys Jones and the production team. Before each ad, the producers would spend months looking through old movies for scenes that could be reconstructed – and incorporate the all-important product. New lines were written for Rhys Jones' character that could be combined with the original scripts; then set designers were brought in to build sets that were replicas of the originals. Not surprisingly, each ad was a complicated shoot. Rhys Jones recalls having to do up to 75 takes of some shots. 'And they go on about Stanley Kubrick needing 45 takes...that's nothing!' he says: 'It's a very intensive process and ten times longer than any other advert I've worked on.'

53 SUGAR PUFFS
HONEY MONSTER 1976

And now for a football teaser. Which 24-year-old has scored a winning goal for Newcastle United *and* saved a penalty for Manchester United? The answer is an eight foot, yellow monster whose post-match quote could only be: 'Tell 'em about the honey, mummy.' John Webster's inspiration for the Sugar Puffs' Honey Monster was a TV series called *The Andy Williams Show* and a character called the Cookie Monster who would bash on Andy's door shouting: 'Cookies! I want cookies!'

Webster borrowed the idea and created a monster who craved honey. The Andy Williams role went to veteran comedy actor Henry McGee, who somehow became the Honey Monster's 'mummy' – despite McGee's protestations of innocence: 'I'm not his mummy!' (Well, they do share the same initials.) 'I wanted a straight man and Henry was one of the straightest of straight men,' recalls Webster. The early ads showed the pyjama-clad McGee explaining to young viewers the exciting benefits of Sugar Puffs, when suddenly the Honey Monster bursts onto the scene – usually by falling through the ceiling or crashing in through a hole in the wall. 'Honey! Honey! I want honey!' he'd growl – and promptly get it via a bowl of Sugar Puffs. The ads soon became as popular as Chopper bikes and Action Men among boys of a certain age, and McGee and his 'adopted son' were opening supermarkets and making other personal appearances.

On one public appearance, an over-enthusiastic youngster stuck a knife into him. Fortunately, the man inside wasn't hurt. 'It wasn't as if there was anything malicious about it, strange as it may seem,' says McGee. 'It was just this funny effect it had on a certain type of child.' Perhaps in an attempt to make him the sort of 'boy' so fascinated by him, the makers of Sugar Puffs changed the monster's image in the eighties. In the space of three years it managed to score a winning goal for Newcastle United at Wembley, save a crucial penalty in a European cup final for Manchester United, and sing with the Irish boy band Boyzone.

52 **HOMEPRIDE**
FLOUR MEN **1965**

Until 1965 Homepride flour was advertised by real-life chefs performing cooking demonstrations. When it became clear that the commercials were making no real difference to sales, a new idea was called for. Ironically, it was to be two Americans, Bob Geers and Bob Gross, who created a TV animation campaign that felt distinctly British. It featured a group of cartoon flour graders in bowler hats, led by a man called Fred (whose voice was provided by *Dad's Army* star John Le

Mesurier). The graders' job was to sort out the grains behind the scenes 'because graded grains make finer flour', as Le Mesurier kept telling us. One famous ad from 1966 – an 'actual scientific demonstration', it said on screen – showed the graders testing flour with a sieve. The rival flour was too lumpy to go through but Homepride passed through with ease, burying a bowler-hatted figure standing underneath.

Soon, sales took off and the little men started to receive fan mail. By 1969 the first ever 'Fred merchandise' came out in the not unexpected form of a flour shaker – made by Airfix and sold for 3/6 and two special tokens. Half a million people sent off for them. Fred has since become something of an advertising cult hero, appearing in nearly 300 ads, and voiced (since John Le Mesurier's death) by actors Joss Ackland and Richard Briers. By 1979 the collector could buy everything from a Fred salt and pepper set to a Fred pocket radio and Fred oven gloves – all of which are much sought after at car boot sales and antiques fairs. Indeed, Fred products are said to have become particularly popular with Japanese tourists who scour shops to find this figure dressed in typically British attire. Not surprisingly, Fred now has his own memorabilia website to add to his fan club.

51 DULUX
DULUX DOG **1968**

Animals have played an important role in advertising over the last 45 years, but few animal-based campaigns have lasted as long as the Dulux dog. Despite early worries, the campaign has proved it has legs – 28 of them, on seven dogs, over 32 years. In one survey four out of five members of the public associated the dog with the right brand. What Old English Sheepdogs have to do with paint is a mystery, but ICI believe that the dog embodies elements of its product's 'personality' – it is warm, friendly and (being a pedigree) full of aspiration.

The Dulux dog was first used in 1961 when an art director included a grey and white Old English Sheepdog in a press advertisement. Seven years later, the idea was transferred to television in the form of Dash, the first Dulux dog, who received £250, a silver food bowl and a year's supply of dog food for his hard work. Dash also had a life outside TV, putting in a number of personal appearances and even appearing in the *Morecambe and Wise Show* as The Amazing Ventriloquist Dog.

In 1974 a dog called Digby won a nationwide competition to find Dash's successor, beating 450 other dogs. He worked with the TV animal trainer Barbara Woodhouse for the campaign. 'Beautiful but not very bright,' was how Woodhouse remembered him. But Digby got the last laugh, meeting the Queen, travelling in chauffeur-driven cars, and becoming the inspiration for the title of the popular children's film *Digby, The Biggest Dog In The World*. Unfortunately, filming commitments meant that Digby couldn't take part.

Digby's replacement, Duke, was the Dulux dog for ten years. Apparently, when Woodhouse wasn't present, Duke would take instructions from her via a tape recorder. Having appeared as 'one of the family' for many years, the Dulux dog took on a leading role in 1991 when (despite the protestations of songwriter Paul Anka) it 'sang' a version of *My Way,* including the lyrics 'And now the end is near, he's finished off the final ceiling.'

50 STELLA ARTOIS
JACQUES DE FLORETTE 1991

Greatly inspired by the French film *Jean de Florette,* director Michael Seresin travelled to Provence to shoot this ad for the 'reassuringly expensive' brand of lager. Seresin, a New Zealander influenced by both Truffaut and Fellini, was also responsible for the long-running Papa/Nicole ad for Renault. This beautifully-shot commercial featured a carnation grower (on his way to market with his donkey and his produce) who is forced to sell a few of his flowers to pay for lunch in a local hostelry. Then, when we see he has also 'bought' a pint of Stella Artois the camera pulls out to reveal the exterior of the building covered in the man's entire hoard of red carnations. 'Stella Artois. Reassuringly expensive,' was the thought we were left with. Although the ad was indeed influenced by *Jean de Florette,* the ad makers used a completely different filming location, as the original settings were considered unsuitable.

They did, however, hire a French 'gofer' who had worked on the original film. Fortunately, he still had in his possession several thousand silk carnations which he had kept under his bed. He was able to hire them out – at a price.

49 HEINZ BEANS
A MILLION HOUSEWIVES 1967

'A million housewives a day pick up a tin of beans and say "Beanz Meanz Heinz".' Surely both improbable and factually incorrect, this is still one of the most famous lines in ad history. Heinz first advertised its beans in 1914 with a slogan aimed at Boy Scouts – 'The best beans for a hike.' Anything would have been an improvement – but 'Beanz Meanz Heinz' wasn't just any slogan.

In 1999, when the slogan was voted 'Most Popular Advertising Slogan Ever', copywriter Mo Drake from Young & Rubicam told *The Mail on Sunday* that he took his team to The Victoria pub in Camden when they failed to come up with an idea for the Heinz campaign. 'I was just scribbling on my pad when it dawned on me that you could end "Beans" with a "Z", as "Heinz" did. Then it came to me – "Beanz Meanz Heinz".' The actual number of housewives who bought Heinz beans each day was 1.75 million. The figure wasn't very 'ad friendly', though, so they knocked it down to a million – a rare case of an agency 'underselling' the product it was promoting.

The new Heinz slogan took some criticism from schoolteachers, who claimed that the company was teaching bad spelling. But thanks to Drake, everyone now knows that Heinz produces 57 varieties – even though, if the truth be told, the company was said to be producing over 60 when the slogan was written. (Heinz reckoned '57' had more of a ring to it than '60'.)

By the eighties, baked beans were the unlikely vehicle for political satire. Set in the thirties, one satirical ad featured a mother making beans for her daughter. The girl asks if eating beans will help her become Prime Minister one day. 'It just might, Margaret, it just might,' says her mother – and realising the implications, she snatches the plate away. The ad ran for six months and saw a massive rise in sales. It was then spoofed in comedy sketch shows – one showing a young Neil Kinnock, with the mother's punchline changed to 'Not a chance in hell'. In the nineties, Drake predicted that a replacement slogan 'Heinz Buildz Britz', wouldn't last 30 years, unlike its predecessor. He was right. It didn't last three.

48 MILK TRAY
AND ALL BECAUSE THE LADY LOVES **1968**

James Bond has a lot to answer for. He inspired the Milk Tray man, eerily dressed in black, to break into women's boudoirs, leaving a calling card and a box of chocolates. These days his photofit would be on *Crimewatch*, but in the old days he was an advertising hero. Milk Tray chocolates first came on to the market in 1915 in open boxes on wooden trays. By the late sixties the design was changed – presumably to avoid spillage while jumping off cliff tops and narrowly avoiding avalanches. The Milk Tray Man came about in 1968; prior to this Cadbury's had focused on the usual present-giving aspects of buying chocolates.

The first man in black was model Gary Myers, who took on much of the stunt work himself. Despite taking on other roles – he played the part of Captain Lew Waterman in the TV series *UFO* – Myers was to carry on jumping off bridges on to moving trains for 20 years until he retired and moved back to Australia, leaving only unanswered questions behind him. Broadcaster Stuart Maconie thinks that the Milk Tray Man was one in a long run of British espionage scandals. 'Just after the Second World War there was Philby, Burgess and McClean and all these scandals in British intelligence,' he says. 'Nowadays in intelligence circles they all get drunk in tapas bars and leave their laptops around with national secrets on them. In the seventies the scandal seemed to be that, instead of getting on with espionage, they were chiefly delivering chocolates to this woman who must have lived in the mountain kingdom of Butan. Where does this woman live that she was only accessible by a combination of helicopter, jet ski and aquafoil?'

Although the theme tune has stayed the same since 1968 (composed as a sub-James Bond affair by Cliff Adams) the ads have evolved, while still retaining the end voice-over: 'And all because the lady loves Milk Tray.' In the year 2000, the ad makers introduced a Milk Tray Girl – model Sienna Guillory – who played a famous film star appearing at a gala event to which her admirer (Milk Tray Man, Hugh Grant-style) has no ticket. Her words 'And where do you think you're going?' were the first spoken by a woman in a Milk Tray add for 32 years. And to think she didn't even thank him for all those chocolates.

47 MATES CONDOMS
CHEMIST SHOP 1988

In 1988 Britain was in the midst of a public health campaign that highlighted the dangers of AIDS. Government-funded ads had hit the airwaves two years earlier, showing a couple in bed, a tombstone and the slogan 'Don't Die Of Ignorance'. In short, Britain seemed doomed unless it changed its ways. But the first Mates ad was a total contrast. It didn't mention AIDS, and it used humour to deliver a serious message. The 'Chemist Shop' commercial was Richard Branson's attempt to break the

Oh no! It's a woman.

virtual monopoly that Durex had in the condom market. This was Virgin trying to get in on the act, as well as an impressive effort to break the taboo of buying condoms, when one could be the difference between life and death.

The commercial showed a young man walking into a high street chemist's, intent on buying a packet of condoms. However, when he sees an attractive, female assistant behind the counter, his courage deserts him. 'I want some...er...some...co...cotton wool, please,' he says. The shop assistant (played by Gina McKee, who was to rise to fame in the BBC series *Our Friends In The North*) seems to know what's going on but, even so, she's quite content to let the youth writhe with embarrassment. 'Have you got a packet of...er...a pack of...er...a packet of tissues please?' he asks. A voice-over then provides the advertisers' real message. 'Mates are a new range of condoms. Like other condoms, they're reliable but they're also cheaper. She sells hundreds of packets. She's not embarrassed so why should you be?'

Eventually the youth picks up the courage to ask for what he came in for – at which point the assistant shouts to the back of the shop, 'Mr Williams, how much for this packet of Mates Condoms?' Within six months of the ad being shown every one in four condoms sold was a Mates condom. 'I think it probably did help to alleviate the embarrassment surrounding buying condoms,' says TV presenter Kate Thornton. 'You managed to see the humour in it. It stopped being excruciating and it became quite comical.'

46 MILK
HUMPHREY'S ABOUT 1975

Ad supremo John Webster could have earned the title 'Ad Maker to the Kids' in the seventies for his creation of the Sugar Puffs Honey Monster and the Cresta bear. Another campaign that was to go down well in Britain's playgrounds came along in 1975 when Webster was given the job of turning milk into something trendy. Traditionally, milk had been seen as a sort of medicine – good for bones. The slogan 'Drinka Pinta Milka Day' had entered the vocabulary in the late fifties, even though (just as in the case of 'Beanz Mean Heinz' a decade later) the spelling had incurred the wrath of *Daily Telegraph* readers and Britain's teachers. In 1975 the Milk Marketing Board wanted a campaign that was new and trendy – and not a lecture on health. Webster recalls that he and his partner at the ad agency stayed up late one night trying to come up with ideas that would be particularly appealing to children. 'We dreamt up this thing about the "Humphreys" who were supposed to be little furry creatures that came up and drank milk – that's why they were so healthy,' recalls Webster. 'That developed into "Wouldn't it be better if they pinched your milk? – watch out there's a Humphrey about!" But we still had them on camera as fluffy things. It was a late decision to say "Well suppose we never see them?"'

A Humphrey was therefore turned into an imaginary creature who would sneak up on unsuspecting milk drinkers and (always through a red and white straw) suck the milk out of a glass. The campaign ran for two years and led to an outbreak of promotional red and white stripy mugs, T-shirts and beer mats. The theme tune with the words 'Watch out, there's a Humphrey about,' was penned by Mike Batt – the man behind the Wombles' shameless attack on the British pop industry.

45 ONE 2 ONE
WHO WOULD YOU LIKE... 1996

'It's much more interesting than a lot of the history programmes that go out on TV. It conjures up connections that no other form does on British television.' So says Philip Dodd, director of the Institute of Contemporary Arts. Dodd speaks of a campaign that has united some unlikely 'couples' over the past few years, and in doing so has produced some of the most inspiring ads in TV history. When Mercury One2One was launched in 1993, the mobile phone market was in its infancy. In fact, Mercury had only two competitors. But despite its initial appeal – free off-peak local calls – by 1996 Mercury One2One was right at the bottom of the table, and publicity was negative and focused on technical difficulties.

Ad agency Bartle Bogle Hegarty was given the job of turning the company's fortunes around. BBH decided to concentrate on the slogan: 'Who would you like to have a One2One with?' It was a campaign designed to suggest the potential of holding intimate conversations on a mobile phone, and used well-known personalities for interest. The first TV ads appeared in October 1996 when model Kate Moss had a One2One with a young Elvis Presley, and former hostage John McCarthy did so with astronaut Yuri Gagarin. 'Kate2Elvis' featured the model saying: 'If I had a One2One with Elvis, I'd ask him who was his best friend. I'd have been a good friend to him.' It caught the public imagination.

One of the most memorable ads featured footballer-turned-TV-presenter Ian Wright, imagining a One2One with civil rights leader Martin Luther King. Like the other personalities used, Wright was asked to name his own choices. 'Forget what these ads are trying to sell to you,' says Philip Dodd. 'They offer you an Utopian moment, and culture generally is not very Utopian these days – it's sour and it's cynical and it's knowing. Above all, the ads allow you to connect across time.'

In 1997, newspapers reported that One2One's takings had soared by 130 per cent since the campaign began. But the company knew it had really taken off when it was reported that the question: 'Who would you like to have a One2One with?' was set as history homework by a head teacher in Cheshire.

44 ESSO
TIGER 1964

For nearly half a century, the petrol company Esso has been associated with the image of a tiger. But their use of the cuddly but deadly beast has changed dramatically over the decades. It was in 1951 that Esso first featured a tiger in its advertising campaigns. The image of the animal leaping out of the magazine towards the reader was supposed to represent the power of the petrol and the energy produced by it. The campaign led to a debate in parliament about whether the tiger encouraged dangerous driving.

A character called the Esso Blue man popped up in the late fifties and early sixties. At that time, petrol ads all featured pseudo-scientific claims about magic formulae which could make your car run faster and smoother than any other. Esso sought to be different.

In 1964, Esso revived the tiger, coming up with the slogan: 'Put A Tiger In Your Tank'. The black and white ads, set to a jazzy tune, showed zany cars with a cartoon tiger inside, with the tiger sometimes beating on a punch-bag inside the car engine. The idea caught on, and in the mid-sixties two a half million people paid 1s 6d each to buy a fake tiger tail to stick on the back of their car. By 1966 Esso believed the public was getting tired of tiger gags and instigated a campaign to revive interest in it by pretending they were getting rid of it. Every national newspaper picked up the story – the 'Save the Tiger' campaign was launched.

The next turning point came in 1973, when Esso decided to let the public know that it was an investor in North Sea oil. The cartoon tiger was too flippant for such a campaign. This time, the tiger had to be real. They eventually found a tiger handler in Los Angeles who had just trained animals for the film *Where The North Wind Blows*. In fact, two animals were used – called India and Kipling – one for close-ups and one for running shots. Unfortunately, when the crew turned up at the US beach location to shoot, they were met by carloads of locals – they had chosen to film on the day the public was allowed to dig for clams.

The image of the Esso tiger has changed many times since 1951 – it even took on a litter of cubs in the nineties to represent our concerns for our children's future environment – and remains one of the most enduring corporate images in British television advertising.

43 OLD SPICE
SURFER 1977

Some ads seem to get lodged in a time warp in modern British history. The Old Spice aftershave commercial was such an ad. It featured a surfer riding a massive wave in some exotic location (we never found out where but it was obviously not Bridlington) and was set to the equally dramatic sounds of Carmina Burana. For a while, in the mid to late seventies, a bottle of Old Spice could be found in many a musty sock and Y-fronts drawer, including that of broadcaster Stuart Maconie, who was among the adolescent hordes enthusiastically splashing on 'The mark of a man'. 'I grew up, like a lot of men of my generation, falling hook, line and sinker for these adverts and believing that Old Spice was the last word in sophistication,' he explains. 'Then, of course, you wear it for the first time and go out somewhere and it stops everyone in their tracks at 40 yards. Every woman in the room says "Who the bloody hell is wearing Old Spice?"' Old Spice was launched in Britain in 1956, two decades after it was created by William Lightfoot Schultz as a fragrance based on the memory of a jar in which his mother kept cloves, roses, herbs and spices. The ad's famous slogan – 'The mark of a man' – was voiced by Steve Hudson, an actor who back in the sixties had starred in a series of commercials for the Mark Vardy range of men toiletries.

One of the men with rugged good looks who appeared in an Old Spice commercial was a Los Angeles actor called John Perry, father of a young lad called Matthew who was to grow up to star in *Friends*. The Old Spice campaign received the ultimate advertising tribute in the early nineties when a Carling Black Label ad showed a surfer riding a wave right up to the bar of a British pub.

42 VW GOLF
CHANGES 1988

It was 1988. Mrs Thatcher had been in power for nearly a decade. Shoulder pads and big hair were 'in'. Women were seizing the initiative and taking control of their lives. And Volkswagen needed an idea to sell their new car at a time of 'yuppiedom' and rampant materialism. The time for some ad break 'Girl power' had come at last. Cue model Paula Hamilton, angrily exiting her lover's (or now ex-lover's) posh London abode, slamming the door and posting a ring through his letterbox. She rips off her pearl necklace, throws a bracelet away and is about to throw her car keys down the drain when she stops to consider what she is doing. Hamilton, complete with Lady Di hairdo, then has a change of heart, gets into her beloved VW car, wipes the rain off the windscreen and, with a smile, drives away. 'If only everything in life was as reliable as a Volkswagen,' states the end caption. The message was clear – for women of a certain age, the car meant freedom. Everything else could go – the ring, the necklace, the man – but the car was indispensable. Up until that point in its advertising history VW's TV campaigns had featured German cars being dropped from great heights to demonstrate their toughness. But here was a way of inserting a bit of warmth into a foreign product – *and* appealing to women, an important target group for Volkswagen.

The ad was directed by David Bailey and had a soundtrack ('Everybody goes through changes') written by Alan Price. It made a star out of the previously unknown Paula Hamilton who then became known as the 'Volkswagen Girl' – even though this was her only appearance in a VW ad. It was also the latest in a long line of celebrated ads by Volkswagen – or rather ad agencies such as London-based BMP DDB Needham, who made 'Changes'. Back in 1960 it was an American agency, Doyle Dane Bernbach, that made a pioneering ad showing a snowplough driver getting to work in a VW Beetle. 'Ever wonder how the man who drives the snowplough gets to work?' was the ad's now famous line of commentary. Nearly 40 years later VW was still inspiring ad makers to come up with great ideas.

41 CAMPARI
LUTON AIRPORT 1977

No one of a certain age can visit Bedfordshire's premier airport without thinking of this advert – and of actress Lorraine Chase.

Chase starred in a number of ads for Campari but the one everyone remembers features the glamorous Cockney actress in a foreign villa, being chatted up by a poetic toff. 'Were you truly wafted here from Paradise?' he asks. 'Nah. Luton Airport,' is her now legendary riposte. It was the sort of memorable East End oneliner that Del Boy would come up with in *Only Fools And Horses* a few years later – and is said to have virtually doubled sales of Campari overnight. The line caught on to such a degree that a female band called Cats UK gratuitously used it in a novelty song called *Luton Airport,* which reached Number 22 in the British charts in 1979. Psychologist Dr David Lewis believes the ad was a success because it took the popular, glamorous campaign for Martini and turned it on its head. 'It had all the elements of a joke. You set up a situation and when your audience thinks it is in one situation you pull the rug from under its feet,' says Lewis.

In 1977 Campari wanted to change its image and attract a new group of women. Lorraine Chase's character – full of no-nonsense, working-class glam – was exactly the right image. Chase recalls the ad agency 'told us they wanted someone who looked classy but had a regional accent – a sort of naff accent'. The idea was first used in a Campari ad shot in Venice which featured the actress saying 'It's nice 'ere, innit?'. Chase was at a West End cinema when the ad came up on the big screen. 'The whole cinema stood up and clapped. I just died! I thought "This is quite amazing!".' Then came 'Luton Airport', filmed not in Luton, but in Hollywood. Chase admits that the ad changed her life, leading to many stage and screen opportunities – but not every change was welcome. 'When people met me (after the ad) they used to assume I'd be stupid and dim and daft,' she recalls.

Ironically, the success of the Lorraine Chase ads gave Campari problems in the years ahead and sales reportedly dropped from 2.5 million bottles a year in the seventies to 420,000 in the nineties. The ads had made people believe that Campari was 'a sweet drink aimed at women'. In an attempt to prove otherwise, the company brought in Jimmy Pursey, ex-leader of Sham 69, to front a new campaign.

 **TETLEY TEA**
TEA FOLK **1973**

Just as Homepride Flour had its graders, Tetley had its tea folk – and still does. The Homepride and Tetley campaigns have many similarities – not least that both feature animated characters who bring an otherwise dull product to life. Although Tetley had begun advertising its tea on TV in 1956, the Tea Folk first appeared in 1973, presenting 'the 2000 perforations that let the flavour flood out' – and have featured in nearly 70 ads since. If the flour graders were bowler-hatted, middle-class Englishmen, the Tea Folk were their northern factory worker equivalents, whose 'gaffer' had the broad Yorkshire accent of Brian Glover. Their ad agency described them as 'warm, friendly, down-to-earth, hardworking' – presumably all the characteristics they would use to describe the people who buy Tetley tea bags. In the early days of the campaign, the characters were clones of each other with only the 'gaffer' standing out. But over the years, different characters have developed within the group. Just as the Flour Graders lost their leader when John Le Mesurier died, the Tea Folk had to find a new gaffer on the death of Glover – Yorkshire comedian Bobby Knutt. Seventies sitcom star George Layton provided the voice of his sidekick, Sydney. Like 'Fred memorabilia', Tetley Tea Folk items have also proved popular. Over the years 30 million tea folk items have been shifted and are thought to be present in 5 million British homes.

Unlike the Homepriders, the Tea Folk have enjoyed a good sing song and a knees up. This side of the campaign was used to try and boost their image in the South of England where they were traditionally seen as downmarket factory workers – and not much fun. Subsequently, when the film *The Full Monty* came out, the Tea Folk introduced the new 'drawstring bag' to the sounds of *The Stripper* theme from the film. The Beach Boys song *I Get Around* was the soundtrack for round tea bags, and the Tetley Tea tune ('Tetley make tea bags make tea') and dance is based on an old Morris Dancing song.

39 FOSTER'S
PAUL HOGAN **1981**

Australian lager has provided us with some of the most entertaining ads of the eighties and nineties – as the inclusion of Foster's and Castlemaine commercials in this list demonstrates. Aussie comedian Paul Hogan had been a big star in his homeland since 1972 when he finished runner up in the grand final of Australian TV's *New Faces*. A former union rep, lifeguard and rigger on the Sydney Harbour Bridge, Hogan first appeared on TV

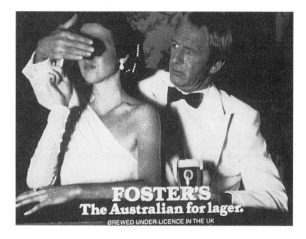

when his workmates dared him to enter the talent show. It was good advice, and a year later he had his own show. *The Paul Hogan Show* featured the comedian as a rules football-loving pub philosopher called Hoges, whose life seemed to revolve around two things – lager and 'the ladies'. (The rather un-PC show was seen over here in the early days of Channel Four in 1982.) In 1981 Hogan started advertising Foster's 'amber nectar' in the UK, in a variety of situations in which he always starred as the innocent abroad – a role he was to repeat to enormous success on the big screen in *Crocodile Dundee* in 1986. Hogan starred as Michael J. 'Crocodile' Dundee, a bush-man who conquers New York with his amiable Aussie ways. It became the most successful Australian film ever made and turned Hogan into a huge star and unofficial roving ambassador for Australia. Hogan's ads for Foster's were also a huge success, making full use of his comic talents and timing, and in the process making Foster's the second biggest-selling lager in Britain.

One of the most popular commercials in the campaign showed Hogan accompanying a glamorous lady to the ballet, while still keeping hold of his true love – a pint of Foster's. All goes well until he sees a male dancer pirouette across the stage in front of them. 'Strewth! There's a bloke down there with no strides on!' says Hogan with surprise, as he covers his lady friend's eyes with his hand. The ad was directed by American Bob Brooks, who was also responsible for other comic classics including the Smash Martians campaign and George Cole's famous ad for B&H small cigars.

38 APPLE
1984 **1984**

Some think this was the greatest ad ever made. It was certainly one of the most ambitious – and talked about. The commercial for Apple's new revolutionary Macintosh computers was made by Ridley Scott, just after he'd completed the futuristic *Blade Runner*. That, along with *Alien* and *Thelma and Louise*, was a long way from West Hartlepool College of Art, where Scott had studied painting and graphic design – and some distance from Scott's famous Hovis ads.

This commercial showed an army of grey zombies listening to a Big Brother figure on an enormous TV screen. Meanwhile, pursued by 'thought police', a female athlete runs into the great hall with a sledgehammer, swinging it at the screen and smashing it to pieces. Big Brother has suddenly exploded into nothing. 'On January 24th Apple Computers will introduce Macintosh. And you'll see why 1984 won't be like "1984",' came the voice-over. The point was (and it was lost on many who just saw an impressively epic 60 seconds) that Apple's new computers represented individualism and democracy. The ad was based on a headline in the *Wall Street Journal* – 'Why 1984 won't be like 1984' – and was originally made to run just once in its native America, in the middle of the 1984 Super Bowl (at a cost of $500,000). But it was such an 'event' that the ad became a huge talking point and was repeated over and over in America and elsewhere.

Although seen as very much an American ad, '1984' was shot at Shepperton Studios in London, costing $400,000. Despite being the ad that made commercials into 'event television', '1984' was nearly not shown at all. According to US author Bernice Kanner, who wrote *The 100 Best TV Commercials,* Apple was worried that other companies would use the Orwellian theme before its ad aired on 23 January. Even after seeing the ad, Apple's directors were unsure if it would work. One director even asked the agency to sell the airtime it had booked. The agency, Chiat Day, did get rid of one spot, but pretended that they couldn't get rid of the second – a minute-long stretch in the second half of the game. In the event, almost 100 million American viewers saw the ad – nearly one in two US households.

37 FRY'S TURKISH DELIGHT
EASTERN PROMISE 1957

One of the UK's oldest brands of chocolate, Fry's Turkish Delight, has been around since before the First World War. The bar of chocolate that was 'full of Eastern promise' has been seen on television since 1957, when the Turkish Delight woman first set foot in that dusty desert teeming with Rudolph Valentino lookalikes. Even in the fifties, advertisers all understood the strong link between chocolate

and sex. 'Chocolate is the next best thing to sex for most people,' says Rupert Howell, president of the Institute of Practitioners in Advertising. 'Chocolate is that sort of luscious, seductive and rewarding thing – and Turkish Delight was the ultimate expression of that.' Throughout the late fifties and sixties, many Turkish Delight ads showed sheikhs grabbing hold of 'slave women', chucking them on the backs of horses and riding off into the distance. (In fact, the very first ad had such a woman unrolled from a carpet in front of a sheikh. Now that's magic.)

'You can feel your heart miss a beat – it's the sultan's favourite treat,' ran the voice-over. Rupert Howell believes that the 'forbidden pleasure' campaign was rather risqué for its day – and '...started a genre of advertising that went on to be probably best done by Flake – this kind of fantastic notion of gratification and quasi-sexual gratification in chocolate'.

By the seventies, the Turkish Delight woman could sit back and relax as a series of men battled for her approval. In more recent times, Turkish Delight women like Vivienne Tribbeck were asked to film these fantasy chocolate commercials not in the Sahara Desert – but Shepperton Studios. It was too expensive to take the crew to Africa, so Africa came to the crew for the four-day shoot – in the shape of sand, snakes, and computer graphics. At least the ad makers had gone to town on the costumes, asking Vivienne Westwood to design them. Meanwhile, Tribbeck, the eighties face of Turkish Delight, went on to become fashion editor of *Cosmopolitan* magazine.

36 FRUIT AND NUT
FRUIT AND NUT CASE 1977

On the night in 1988 that Frank Muir died, aged 77, the writer, actor and raconteur had been watching the Tom Hanks film *Forrest Gump*. 'Life is like a box of chocolates; you never know what you're gonna get,' was one of Gump's homespun philosophies. The irony was that despite the many TV series and books that Frank Muir was involved in, many people still remember him as the British eccentric standing in a river promoting one of Britain's favourite chocolate bars while singing: 'Everyone's a Fruit and Nut Case.' From 1977 onwards Frank Muir was the face of Cadbury's Fruit and Nut in a series of surreal, Monty Pythonesque commercials. Born in 1920, Muir left school without a single qualification. A clue as to why this might have been comes in his list of hobbies, which included 'staring into space'. Joining the RAF a year after war broke out, Muir was posted to Iceland – where he decided that scriptwriting was his forte. Muir teamed up with Denis Norden, now known as the host of *It'll Be Alright On The Night,* but who was also Muir's comedy writing partner for a number of years.

Muir went on to become head of the BBC's comedy department and in part responsible for series such as *Steptoe and Son* and *Till Death Us Do Part,* before leaving to become LWT's head of entertainment in 1969. In the early seventies, Muir – a distinct-looking and sounding 6ft 5in gent wrapped up in a pink bow tie – was a captain on the BBC parlour game *Call My Bluff*. But he was to reach a new audience a few years later when he appeared in a series of popular ads, singing his catchy jingle. Psychologist Dr David Lewis believes Muir got the intended message across beautifully in a campaign that took more risks than many of us think. 'The commercials were interesting because they had a slightly eccentric message – that everyone is a "fruit and nut case",' says Lewis. 'If you actually took that seriously it would be rather worrying. What they are saying, presumably, is that everybody is rather psychotic! But they are not saying that really…so it was absolutely essential for it to be taken very lightly – as a joke – and not as a serious statement about human society.'

35 MARTINI
ANYTIME, ANYPLACE, ANYWHERE 1970

'Anytime was a Saturday afternoon, anyplace was in Derby where my mother happened to live and I was sitting in a tiny little sitting room in her two up, two down council house with a bit of paper in front of me and her asking me if I wanted any more tea, love?' So reveals Barry Day, creator of the Martini slogan that entered the English language in the seventies. 'You think of these things wherever you can. It doesn't have to be on a beach, it doesn't have to be on a helicopter; it can be anywhere and it frequently is.'

With respect to Derbyshire council houses, the image that Martini drinkers aspired to in those days was more glamorous – like sailing in a hot air balloon over a Spanish castle while having your tipple. The Martini ads showed the 'beautiful people' having a marvellous time while the theme tune – all strings and singers – played in the background.

'Anytime, anyplace, anywhere – there's a wonderful world you can share.
It's the bright taste of the right one – that's Martini.'

Anytime. Anyplace. Anywhere.

Day's job was to come up with an advertising campaign that showed 'thirtysomethings' (as they came to be called) conquering the world by having a glass of Martini – instead of a beer or a glass of Babycham. 'It was like trying to sell a cosmetic in the shape of a glass,' says Day. 'Our idea was to make it the most beautiful drink in the world, and take advantage of the desire to see the rest of the world,' he says. 'Young people at that time had not really travelled widely – they hadn't got the money – but they wanted to. So [we thought] why don't we create this jetset world and let people go into it in our commercials, and show the people drinking the stuff in all sorts of glamorous settings?'

Getting a part in a Martini ad must have been a great gig – they were always filmed in glamorous locations and had plenty of money spent on them.

34 PEPSI
LIPSMACKINTHIRSTQUENCHIN' 1973

Lipsmackinthirst
quenchinacetast
inmotivatingood
buzzincooltalkin
highwalkinfastliv
inevergivin
coolfizzin

A Radio Luxembourg DJ was the influence behind this ad for a product which hasn't always proved lucky for those advertising it. Seeing a pretty, blonde woman by a swimming pool a young nerd of a man gathers up the courage to go and speak to her. He launches into a long, stuttering, embarrassed monologue about how he saw the girl and wondered whether she might fancy a Pepsi. As he finishes the girl replies – in *Swedish,* obviously not having understood a single word. The ad ends with a burst of *movin', groovin'* rock music – and perhaps the longest slogan in British advertising history:

'Lipsmackin-thirstquenchin-acetastin-motivatin-goodbuzzin-cooltalkin-highwalkin-fastlivin-evergivin-coolfizzin...Pepsi.'

'It was influenced by a chap called Emperor Roscoe who was a DJ who used to make up these long words,' says John Webster, who was the art director on the ad. Webster saw it as a way of getting through to teenagers of the day, and turned the star of the ad into an anti-hero. 'It was the time of *The Graduate* with Dustin Hoffman and suddenly the anti-hero was the hero,' says Webster. 'He didn't get the girl. But everyone sympathised with him.' It was a funny, low-budget way of promoting Pepsi – but not typical of the Pepsi ads that were to come in the following decades.

In the eighties and nineties Pepsi used pop stars like Michael Jackson, Madonna, Ray Charles and The Corrs to move their product. But despite the huge sums they no doubt received for promoting it, Jackson and Madonna had reason to wonder whether it was all worth it. Madonna's 1989 ad was dropped after complaints that *Like A Prayer* – the song used on the ad – was blasphemous, while Jackson's hair famously caught fire while filming his Pepsi ad in 1984. It makes a minor understanding with a Scandinavian girl seem such a piddling little thing.

33 JOHN SMITH'S BITTER
DOG TRICKS **1981**

Peter Tinniswood's *I Didn't Know You Cared* had been a popular BBC sitcom since 1975 about life with a dour Yorkshire family. John Webster was a fan. 'I loved the humour in it – this flat, Yorkshire humour that appealed to Southerners,' he recalls.

It was the inspiration for a whole series of ads promoting a Northern beer outside its native Yorkshire. Gordon Rollings, who had played Minnie Caldwell's lodger in *Coronation Street,* played the part of Arkwright – a flat-capped stereotypical Northerner 'who sees life in terms of beer', according to Webster. But the real star was Arkwright's dog. 'We had a huge casting, with about a hundred dogs,' says Webster. 'The one we chose was a Jack Russell we called Tonto. He wasn't trained but he made you laugh just to look at him.'

On the first day of filming the first ad, Tonto was required to perform a number of tricks, enticed by his owner with the words: 'Fancy a drop of John Smith's?' (Arkwright's drinking pal, Stan, had said his new dog was boring.) At the mention of a pint, Tonto juggles some balls, balances a bar stool on his nose, jumps into the air and stands on his head. 'He just needs the right motivation,' says Arkwright.

Webster explains: 'There was a juggler on his knees behind the bar, juggling. When Tonto's back legs came up that was a stuffed dog with levers. When Tonto jumped up in the air, we had four men and a blanket tossing him up in the air.' Tonto's tricks were filmed separately, fitting into a gap between the two drinking pals at the bar. It had all gone well until the ad makers got the developed film back. They'd made the mistake of sending it to the lab on two different nights – the result being that the colour of the pub wall behind the dog changed throughout the series of tricks.

They might have noticed, but no one else did. The campaign was an instant success in the South of England. 'It sort of fulfilled people's ideas of what a typical northerner was like,' says Webster. 'But in the North it didn't go down well at all. They didn't think of themselves like that. So it was completely rejected up there – we had to devise a completely new campaign for them.'

32 DURACELL
BUNNY 1975

The words 'pink', 'bunnies' and 'drum kit' don't often go together in daily conversation but certain ad men seem to have done little else but link the three. Of all the 'pink bunny with a drum kit' ads, the 'Energizer' bunny is probably the most famous worldwide. Its drumming antics (allegedly three times longer than those of any other drumming, pink rabbit) made it an advertising icon in the US. That particular bunny has appeared in over a hundred ads, a series of spoofs, cartoons and political campaigns – and has even had chat show host David Letterman club it with a baseball bat. But Energizer didn't produce the first rabbit. That credit must go to to Duracell.

In 1980, after Duracell dropped the campaign in the USA, Eveready, the makers of Energizer, picked up the baton (or drumstick) and ran like hell. Students of the advertising 'drummer bunny' will point out a world of difference between the Duracell and Energizer rabbits. Although both are pink and rabbits, this is where the similarities end. The original Duracell bunny was like a child's cuddly toy with a snare drum. By contrast the Energizer bunny wore dark glasses and marched with a big bass drum. Berny Stringle, who directed the classic PG Tips chimps ads, is a man who knows a thing or two about pink, drumming bunnies. If he had thought filming piano-playing chimps was hard, that turned out to be a tea party compared with the Duracell shoot. 'The most frustrating thing about it was that it did go on and on and on, but it just kept falling over, just at the moment when everything else in the scene was perfect,' Stringle remembers. So did he have to change batteries? 'Absolutely did we have to change batteries! I mean, it wasn't so much that the battery wouldn't do it – it just wouldn't stand up. At the end of it though the ad looked great.' The Duracell bunny has become something of a collector's item in recent years. Fans of the Duracell pink bunny can buy not just a drumming bunny, but also a skiing bunny, a canoeing bunny and a 1998 World Cup footballing bunny. Football is all well and good but what a rival company did in 1999 simply wasn't cricket. At the height of the 'battery wars' a TV ad for Grandcell Batteries showed a lifeless, pink rabbit (remarkably similar to our cuddly Duracell hero) under a sheet on an autopsy table.

31 GOLD BLEND
COUPLE 1987

By the eighties it was cool to watch TV soaps. However, one of the best known TV soap romances of the eighties wasn't in Brookside Close, Albert Square or even in Texas – it was acted out in a flat somewhere in London. Nescafé Gold Blend was introduced in the mid-sixties. For the next 20 years the ad campaigns would focus on the product itself. Then the ad agency changed tack, focusing instead on what Gold Blend could do for you – make you into a successful, sophisticated person of the eighties. It was onto a winner.

One of the campaign's influences was the American TV series *Moonlighting*, which featured a 'Will they, won't they?' romantic sub-plot around stars Bruce Willis and Cybill Shepherd. The plot appealed to the women who were the target audience for Gold Blend, so the makers of the new ads decided to mimic the show, ending each episode on a cliffhanger. The campaign was the making of its stars Anthony Head and Sharon Maughan. Maughan got the part while recovering from the birth of her second child. 'I wasn't

well and I had eczema on my face,' recalls Maughan. 'I couldn't believe anyone was asking me to do something wherein they would make me look better. I thought it might be my only shot, because I wasn't feeling very confident.'

The risk paid off. When Tony Head knocked on the door of Maughan's flat in November 1987, introduced himself, and asked if he could borrow her coffee, the combination of good looks and sophistication was an instant hit with millions of viewers. At one stage their romance merited an editorial in *The Times*.

By the time the search was on for the new Gold Blend couple, over 4,000 women applied. The role was given to Louise Hunt. Her partner in caffeine was actor Mark Aitken. The third Gold Blend couple – Simone Bendix and Neil Roberts – were the final lovers to take the roles. Many ads have produced spin-offs, but Gold Blend is the only product to have its own CD of love songs (*Love Over Gold* – which went top ten), a video of the ad campaign and a bestselling novel.

All this can be forgiven because the campaign achieved what it set out to – it pushed sales of up Gold Blend by 70 per cent, and in doing so helped it grow from a minor player to the second biggest coffee brand in the UK.

30 KIT KAT
PANDAS **1989**

Kit Kat was first produced in 1935 as Rowntrees Chocolate Crisp, but changed its name two years later. It is supposedly named after the Kit Kat Club – an 18th century Whig club made up of writers and politicians. (Though what they have to do with chocolate fingers, heaven only knows.). Early ads featured a character called Kitty The Kat but the famous slogan – 'Have a break, have a Kit Kat' was first used in a TV commercial in 1957. Perhaps the best Kit Kat ad came 22 years later. A wildlife photographer waits patiently with his camera pointed towards a pandas' enclosure in a zoo. Through wind and rain, night and day, he stands waiting to get a shot of the pandas emerging from their home. Alas, nothing happens. Finally, deciding he needs a break, the photographer takes a Kit Kat out of his coat pocket, turns around with his back to the enclosure and starts to eat it. As soon as his back is turned, the pandas creep out of their home and perform a series of stunts, like dancing and skating to the strains of music that sound like something from the Blackpool Tower Ballroom in *Come Dancing*.

Having finished their impressive routine, the photographer, oblivious to all this, turns back towards the enclosure and stands there, hands on his camera, waiting. The Panda ad provided one of the funniest spots of the late eighties, but other Kit Kat ads have also worked well, including one which featured a pair of road painters whose white lines go askew due to their chocolate consumption. The painters weren't alone in their Kit Kat habit. According to the makers of the chocolate bar, 47 Kit Kats are eaten every second.

29 HEINEKEN
REFRESHES THE PARTS 1974

Up until this famous campaign, beer ads usually featured three blokes in a pub. Heineken broke the mould. Collett Dickenson Pearce won the brief to sell Heineken on TV. The agency's instructions were just that – *brief*. 'All we got was a yellow card, and it said: "Heineken – foreign – requirement – refreshment." That was about it,' recalls Terry Lovelock, the writer who worked on the campaign.

Lovelock and his art director partner Vernon Howe had three weeks to come up with an idea. Two and a half months later, Howe went off to the Atlas Mountains to do a shoot for Ford, and Lovelock decided to go

with him. 'One night I woke up at three o'clock,' recalls Lovelock. 'I always kept a pen and paper near the bed. I wrote down two lines. One was "Heineken refreshes the parts others cannot reach", the other left out any reference to "the parts".' (He thought the advertising authorities might veto 'parts'.) The resulting ad was tested on the public and failed – probably because it was so far removed from beer ads of the past. Still, with courageous backing from the client, the agency went ahead.

Early Heineken ads were simple but effective – a piano tuner failing to tune a piano until he has had a drop of Heineken; the tired feet of bobbies becoming refreshed after a glass. Actor Victor Borge was brought in for the voice-over.

One of the most celebrated Heineken ads (directed by Paul Weiland) was a 1986 pastiche of the George Bernard Shaw scene from *Pygmalion* which featured the lines 'The rain in Spain...'. The agency wanted a Sloane Ranger saying these lines – posh at first and then with a more and more working-class accent as she sips the Heineken. Then, at the eleventh hour, it emerged that the lines would cost a fortune to clear – so the ad team had to use their imagination – and fast.

In a flash of brilliance, they came up with 'The water in Majorca don't taste like what it oughta'. In this case, according to Borge, it was Heineken refreshing the parts *wot* other beers cannot reach. Another ad featured Wordsworth failing to come up with: 'I wandered lonely as a cloud'. 'I walked around a bit,' he begins. After two decades and 100 variations on a theme, Heineken ended its classic campaign in 1990 with lonely shopping trolleys returning from their resting places – fields and river banks included – to the supermarket from whence they all came. It was a perfect ending for one of British advertising's all-time greats.

28 HOVIS
BIKE RIDE **1974**

Filmed by Ridley Scott, and set to the sounds of Dvorak's *New World Symphony,* the Hovis boy pushing his bike up the hill is one of the most enduring images in British advertising history. The ad feels distinctly British – distinctly *Yorkshire* in fact. But despite having a Yorkshire actor voicing the part of the boy looking back at his daily task; despite having brass band music all over it; and despite featuring Yorkshireman Bill Maynard as the baker, the ad had nothing to do with Yorkshire at all. In fact, it was filmed on Gold Hill, in Shaftesbury, Dorset – where a gold loaf still stands to tell tourists they're standing on the top of advertising history.

In 1974, at a time of industrial action and three-day weeks, ad makers Collett Dickenson Pearce opted to exploit nostalgia to persuade viewers that Hovis was better than its competitors.People buying Hovis were buying a valuable piece of the past, was the clear message. 'The Hovis ad is a most fantastic 30-second social document,' says cultural historian Robert Hewison. 'It was made just after the oil crisis. There had been miners' strikes, industrial unrest and racial tension and the whole of Britain was starting to worry about its identity. What happens at those times is that people reach for the security blanket of the past.' Hovis had been produced since 1885 – the name is short for *Hominis Vis,* meaning strength of man – and CDP wanted to stress that the product still had good old-fashioned values. In fact they wanted to say Hovis was 'good for you' but, due to advertising restrictions, had to settle for: 'As good today as it's always been.'

The Ridley Scott ad is often cited as one of the first to change the way we perceived TV commercials. It had all the values of a mini movie – the lighting, the soft focus camera work and the thoughtful soundtrack. Add to that nostalgic charm and, suddenly, commercials could be art too.

There were other commercials in the same campaign – including one showing a soldier coming home from the First World War. But none were able to surpass the sight of young Carl Barlow (now a London fireman) coming out of the gleaming sun and up that hill. The ad was shown for an astonishing 19 years.

27 MILKY BAR
THE MILKY BAR KID 1961

Since the sixties the Milky Bar Kid campaign has managed to support small, pale, freckly boys with poor vision. All they needed to do if bullied at school was fire an imaginary pistol and shout: 'The Milky Bars are on me!' and all would be forgiven. Indeed, Michael Mayne, who was one of the first Milky Bar kids and was seen shooting bullets through playing cards, reckons he was something of a trendsetter. 'I think I was probably the first "normal" child on television. I had NHS glasses on,' he says. 'Until then, most of the children on TV were absolutely perfect. The idea of having someone who is all-powerful and can do anything *and who* wears glasses was absolutely brilliant.'

Nestlé launched the Milky Bar in Switzerland in 1937 but it survived without its hero until 1961. Since then, 15 youngsters have taken on the role of the 'kid' since Terry Brooks (who went on to run an air-conditioning business in Basildon) first stepped into his cowboy boots. He quit the role after six years, for personal reasons. 'I had got to an age where girls were coming on the scene. You don't want to be the Milky Bar Kid when you're trying to chat up the birds,' he told the *Evening Standard* in 1993. From Wild West saloons to Star Wars scenarios the backgrounds might have changed over the decades, but the persona of the 'kid' has stayed the same. Mind you, the ad makers have had to cheat a bit. John Cornelius took on the role a decade after Michael Mayne but had perfect eyesight. 'I didn't wear glasses. They put glasses on me,' he reveals 30 years on. Not only that but he didn't even like the taste of Milky Bars. ' It was like "Cut!" and then I'd spit it into a cup,' he says. Britain isn't the only country to have experienced the Milky Bar Kid. In New Zealand, a series of different child actors have stepped into his cowboy boots since the sixties. Sadly, the original 'kid' in New Zealand was killed three years ago at the hands of a gunman. Ironically, guns had been banned from Milky Bar ads by Nestlé.

26 FLAKE
FLAKE GIRLS **1959**

Since 1959 Cadbury's have delivered a series of ads that have become known as 'phallic classics', involving beautiful women (often shot against lots of sun) wandering through poppy fields, sailing under waterfalls and cooling off on window sills while eating a six-inch piece of flaky chocolate. 'You can guess someone's age by their favourite Flake commercial,' says Trevor Beattie, who made a Flake ad in 1999 to celebrate the bar's 40th anniversary. 'Everyone has a favourite because it happened at a particularly adolescent time of their life.'

The now-famous Flake was invented by accident in 1911 when a machine operator realised the folds of chocolate left on the side of the moulding machine could be put to good use. Despite the phallocentric nature of the ads, Cadbury's says its target consumers are women aged 16-34 who see Flake as escapism.

However, Trevor Beattie (who is neither female nor between 16 and 34) cites *his* favourite Flake ad as the one where the girl with spiky black hair sinks into a bath as the music fades away. According to Beattie, Flake ads have always been loaded with sexual symbolism – way back to the early sixties when it was advertised as 'sixpence worth of heaven'. Even the appearance of a lizard shuffling across a ringing telephone had some sort of erotic significance – though no one knows quite what. 'The idea of the lizard on the telephone came from the lighting cameraman who said "Why don't we add this touch of exotica?", says Beattie. 'When we researched the film (the 1999 Flake retrospective), women said: "Yeah, we like the lizard – and we are not going to tell you why."'

Lizard or no lizard, model-turned-actress Deborah Leng still managed to hit the headlines in the tabloids for her steamy portrayal of the Flake girl. Sitting on a windowsill in what looked like a French château she made an 'error' while filming her part. 'When I bit it [the Flake] I put my tongue on it, which was a "no-no" – this I only found out after the commercial came out,' she says. 'I was quite embarrassed and there was a lot of press because it was very sexy. But sales went up dramatically.' According to Beattie, the way the Flake crumbles is very important: 'It has to crumble by its nature – it's essential to a Flake commercial,' he says. Above all, the Flake must be brushed off the lips. 'Absolutely essential,' he adds.

25 CASTLEMAINE
SHERRY **1986**

Paul Hogan and Foster's had set the way for stereotypical Aussie lager ads in the eighties – and Castlemaine took up the can and ran with its: 'Australians wouldn't give a Castlemaine XXXX for anything else' slogan. Indeed, if anything, the Castlemaine ads were even funnier than those for Foster's. Watney's, the company that launched Foster's in 1981, must have thought they'd cornered the market when they linked Australian man with canned lager. So Allied Brewers, the producers of Castlemaine, were taking something of a risk with their similar advertising strategy, which they launched in 1984. However, the risk paid off and by 1987 Castlemaine had become one of the bestselling lagers in the UK.

In one of the best ads of the campaign Saatchi and Saatchi went to the desert of New South Wales to film a party of sheepshearers about to get on the road and head for a party. Broken Hill, the film location, was chosen because it was one of the few places in Australia where camera crews could film in the desert without planes buzzing overhead. The macho sheepshearers are seen loading their dilapidated pickup van with pack after pack of Castlemaine lager. Suddenly it occurs to them to take something for 'the ladies'. One of the shearers picks up two bottles of sweet sherry and puts them on the back of the van – at which point the vehicle lets out a loud groan and collapses on its back wheels.

'Looks like you've overdone it on the sherry,' says one of his colleagues without the slightest hint of irony.

24 PG TIPS
CHIMPS **1956**

In the fifties the scientist Arthur C. Clarke predicted that we would be using chimps as servants by 2000. Okay, so they're not taking dictation and loading the dishwasher, but they did conquer one difficult task – turning PG Tips into a brand leader. 'Do you know the piano's on my foot? You hum it – I'll play it' has been shown on British TV over a thousand times.

However, the chimps campaign had been going for 15 years before the removal 'men' hit our screens. The idea of using chimps to sell tea came to copywriter Rowley Marsh in 1955 after he saw a chimps' tea party at London Zoo. A year later, the first ad was shot around a dinner table in a stately home. The crew filmed everything the animals did and Peter Sellers provided the voices. The first ad was shown on Christmas Day 1956. Three years later, PG Tips was at the top spot, helped by a budget of nearly £700,000.

By 1969, PG Tips were looking for ways to take the campaign forward. In 1971, everything changed when the wife of ad director Berny Stringle had a glass of red wine spilled over her on a flight. The drink-spilling passenger worked for the agency that produced the PG Tips ads, and was looking to make them more script led. The two men got talking. 'I'd just seen a Laurel and Hardy film, the one where they are shifting a piano,' recalls Stringle. 'He'd figured that things that were corny would have great appeal coming out of the mouths of chimps.' Scriptwriter Tony Toller was brought in and Stringle asked to direct. By coincidence, Stringle had been teaboy on the very first chimps' ad shoot.

It was not until Stringle arrived at Shepperton Studios on the first day of shooting that he realised what he'd got himself into. 'I suddenly realised I'd got a storyboard and a script and I knew exactly what I wanted to do – and I was faced with some wild animals that I couldn't talk to,' says Stringle. 'Because of the love between the trainer and the animals I recognised that they would do things for these trainers. But they didn't always look in the right direction when they did it.'

But could they *really* film such ads without being cruel to the chimps? Stringle is adamant. 'You can't push them too far because they won't work after that. If a chimp gets in a bad temper it's just not going to play ball.'

23 CORNETTO
JUST ONE CORNETTO **1980**

Legend has it that the ad team at Lowe Lintas were working on a totally different idea for Walls' Cornetto when the ice cream company changed its mind and asked the agency to come up with something new. The result was a spot based around the song *O Sole Mio* – and one of the most popular and spoofed ads of the early eighties. 'A little piece of Italy for only a shilling' was the slogan that had been used to promote Cornetto in 1965. Although the idea flopped first time round it came back with a clever new (and musical) angle a decade and a half later. The first and most famous ad in the new campaign was shot in Venice and showed a gondolier snatching the Cornetto of a passer-by. 'Just one Cornetto, give it to me, delicious ice cream from Italy,' were the words sang to the tune of *O Sole Mio* by Renato, one half of the duo Renée and Renato, famous in Britain for their novelty number one *Save Your Love*.

It was a simple idea but one whose 'naff cheek' seemed to strike a chord with the viewers – and other ad makers. Barclaycard and Boddingtons spoofed the idea – the latter consisted of a shoot on a canal in the middle of Manchester. So what was its appeal? Psychologist Dr David Lewis has a cruel theory: 'It sets up opera to be the fall guy in a joke by positioning it by very unexpected images,' he says. 'I think for many people this would work quite well because it would be seen as a joke and a lot of people would think that was quite sophisticated. But I think the people who think it is quite sophisticated are probably not, dare I say, terribly sophisticated themselves.'

Walls followed up their famous Gondola ad with a commercial about a traffic cop in Rome.

22 OXO
FAMILY 1958

For nearly half a century TV commercials have reflected British life both as it is, and how we would like it to be, but the Oxo family campaign, which ran for 34 of those years, has demonstrated the changes in British society perhaps more than any other.

During the Second World War Oxo was seen as a value-for-money drink, but in the late fifties the plan was to move it more up-market. Subsequently, a campaign was formed around an attractive, young housewife. Actress Mary Holland became the Oxo mum, Katie, in 1958.

Early ads showed her busy in the kitchen, preparing dinner for her new husband Philip. 'Good girl,' he says, when he sees his wife using Oxo to 'give a meal man appeal', as Katie tells us. It all sounds pretty sexist stuff but back in 1958 (when Katie didn't work and was always immaculately dressed) the public wasn't used to seeing 'real' people in ads. The campaign was an instant hit. 'It worked. A lot of people thought it really did encourage happy families,' recalls Holland.

Men fancied Mary/Katie and women wanted to be like her. Over the next few years Katie became the most-loved character in British advertising – and the first to take on a life of her own. Holland feels that people liked her because she was human – she made mistakes in the kitchen. After one ad, where Philip chastised Katie for crying at a sad film, it was reported in the press that a factory had come to a dead halt while workers debated Philip's beastly behaviour.

Viewers seemed to believe Katie was *real* – a point of view which pleased Oxo, if not Mary Holland, who was required to give interviews on TV *as* Katie. 'For many years they (Oxo) wanted this to continue – that I was Katie and there really was a husband and there really was a little boy,' says Holland. 'Then the bubble burst and it was discovered that I wasn't really Katie and I really did have a husband and other children – real children!'

Having ditched their family and replaced them with actor Dennis Waterman wearing a red T-shirt with 'Oxo' written on it, the company resurrected the family notion in 1983. Immediately it was different to its predecessor – the family argued, stomped upstairs, played loud music and (gasp) seemed to promote feminism and vegetarianism. Katie would have been turning in her gravy.

21 FERRERO ROCHER
AMBASSADOR'S PARTY 1995

Some ads sneaked into *The 100 Greatest TV Ads* by the back door – Shake'n'Vac, Brut, Ferrero Rocher – there's something about them that sets them aside from the Hamlets, Heinekens and Hovises of this world. (You almost feel dirty talking about them in the same paragraph.) And yet, these ads co-existed in our commercial breaks, so why not in a list of the greatest (or perhaps 'most memorable') ads ever? Even if they're not considered great works of 20th-century art,

they have all stuck in our memory like a 50p piece wedged forever in a railway station chocolate machine. No matter how hard you try, you just can't shift it – like the memory of that Shake'n'Vac song and dance routine. Ferrero Rocher was one such campaign – an Italian job looking not unlike an outtake from *Dynasty* and with a keyboard soundtrack like something from a low-budget European porn movie. 'The Ferrero Rocher commercial is one of the great enigmas of modern advertising, because everyone remembers it,' says psychologist Dr David Lewis. 'Everyone thinks it must have some kind of ironic subtext. It is almost *Pythonesque;* you expect the SAS to come crashing through the French windows and disrupt the party. It must be successful because it has been running a long time...but I can't think how it is.'

The campaign featured gatherings of European 'sophisticats' at parties thrown by the Italian Ambassador. At a given point in the evening (presumably the climax) the ambassador snaps his fingers and in walks a servant with a tray piled triangularly high with enough chocolates for the entire nation of Italy. It wasn't clever and it wasn't funny. And yet everyone remembered it for not trying too hard to be either. So were the Italian ad makers being deliberately naff? Or does the campaign just go to show that a single European currency may one day be possible, but as far as ads go, what looks trendy in Turin can look downright silly in Sussex? Still, and for whatever reason, it shifted the chocs in the shops and that's all that mattered. 'The Ambassador's Party was just kitsch beyond belief and there are some ads that pass into that category where people laugh at them, but enjoy them nonetheless,' says Rupert Howell, president of the Institute of Practitioners in Advertising.

20 REAL FIRES
FURRY FRIENDS 1988

In the late eighties the Chamber of Coal Traders wanted to run a campaign to show the benefits of a real fire. Saatchi and Saatchi came up with the idea of three natural enemies – a cat, a dog and a mouse – uniting around the fire. There was only one question: how would they do it? Several directors were interviewed for the job. One suggested using a split screen technique by which the animals would appear together in the final ad but would actually be filmed separately; a second suggested using actors dressed as animals. Only ad supremo Tony Kaye suggested that an ad done for the real thing should be done – for real. 'I have this thing about film-making that children and animals are the best thing,' he says. 'If you use an animal or a child in an appropriate way, you cannot fail. They will smote any actor. They will smote Marlon Brando, they will smote Meryl Streep, because you have the audience in the palm of your hand.'

To make the ad Saatchi and Saatchi cast a cat and a dog from 80 different animals and made them live together for several weeks so they could get used to each other. However, the original cat had to be withdrawn at the last minute so a brand new feline had to be employed. The mouse, by the way, got the job after a rat failed the audition because it made a constant mess on the film set. The commercial shows the bulldog entering the living room first and sitting down in front of a fire. He is followed by a cat which snuggles up next to him (encouraged by a prawn which Kaye placed behind the dog's ear).

Cut to a white mouse which runs into the room, takes a sniff at the cat and then sits down next to the two other animals – all in front of the fire of course. 'Now you know what people see in a real fire' was the message at the end. The entry of the dog and cat didn't prove a problem, but the mouse was more of a challenge. 'You can train cats and dogs but you can't train a mouse,' remarks Kaye. All he could do was sit and wait – and hope for the best. 'I just put the dog and cat together and kept doing it until the mouse just happened to go there. Now and again someone had to dive in and go "phut" [to stop the cat eating the mouse] but I knew that I'd get it because I had all the shots worked out.'

On one occasion Kaye, who was behind the camera filming the countless takes over the course of two days, noticed the mouse taking a sniff at the cat on one take. He decided to include it in the ad as a kiss. Ironically, Kaye suggests that, although the animals got on like a house on, er, fire, the only problems were with the pet owners behind the scenes. 'They were all squabbling about how much they were getting paid, like: "Just because yours is a dog doesn't mean you should get any more than me and my mouse because my mouse is actually just as important to the story as your dog",' he recalls. Anyway, the filming completed, all the ad makers had to do was put the soundtrack on top of the animal antics. Kaye was keen on turning the ad into a sort of love story by using Frank Sinatra's *Strangers In The Night,* but Saatchi and Saatchi had other ideas.

The song that was eventually used was *Will You Still Love Me Tomorrow?,* originally recorded by sixties girl band The Shirelles. The version used in the ad, however, was a re-recorded version using session singers. Something else in the ad wasn't quite what it seemed. It turns out bulldogs don't like sitting near fires because they have respiratory problems. The solution? The fire in the ad wasn't real; the flames reflecting on the animals were all done by a trick of the lighting. However, the bulldog breed did come out of the campaign quite well and suddenly found itself in demand as pets in the late eighties.

Kaye followed up *Furry Friends* with an ad for the same client showing a young boy bathing with a python in front of a fire. The commercial was withdrawn after a fortnight following complaints from viewers.

19 ANDREX
PUPPIES **1972**

'There was a fantastic rule, up until the early sixties, about how you could advertise loo paper on television,' says Rupert Howell. 'Apparently Monday to Saturday you could call it "toilet tissue", but if the ad went out on a Sunday you had to call it "lavatory paper" – because only posh people watched telly on Sundays or something. I mean, it is just bizarre.' Toilet paper has seemingly always been a difficult product to advertise. After all, you can show people drinking Coke, splashing on Brut or downing a pint of John Smith's, but you can hardly show them making best use of a packet of Andrex. Hence, the existence of several generations of cute puppies causing chaos in countless middle-class homes to sell what the ad agency J Walter Thompson call 'a low-interest, low-anxiety product'.

'The secret of the Andrex ad is – how do you talk about something that nobody really wants to talk about?' says Howell.

'The puppies are just a cute analogy for something being soft and acceptable – and I suspect it was something that was stumbled upon and just became popular.' The Andrex Labrador puppies have been running riot since 1972 – a 28-year advertising campaign during which it has been calculated that the animals have used up around 500 miles of toilet paper. (Mind you, that's nothing compared to the one and a half million rolls of the stuff sold in the UK every day.) And yet the famous advertising campaign was indeed stumbled upon and might never have happened if it wasn't for TV advertising watchdogs.

Back in 1972 Andrex planned to use a child unravelling a toilet roll, but the authorities thought it might encourage naughtiness in Britain's easily led astray infants. Instead, the ad agency sold the makers of Andrex a pup that we have come to know and love. J Walter Thompson has had the Andrex account for over 30 years now, during which time Andrex became the first company to produce coloured loo roll. The agency uses puppies aged between five and nine weeks for filming. And, like many TV viewers watching these ads, the puppies have an attention span of around 15 minutes – so over a dozen puppies are used for each commercial.

'The Andrex ads are a real testament to the extraordinary things that British people will find cute,' says broadcaster Stuart Maconie. 'And yet if you look at the raw material of the ad, it doesn't really speak to me of cute. It's got bog roll, whose normal associations are with seventies football hooligans and unpleasant bodily functions; and it's clearly got a mad dog in it who becomes entangled in bog roll and charges through a house knocking over some priceless family heirlooms...and yet everyone is delighted.'

Despite some mystery over *why* we find these ads so enthralling, the Andrex ads are among the most popular ever produced in Britain. Twice (in 1988 and 1991) an Andrex ad has been voted the public's favourite commercial of the year in *Marketing* magazine's Adwatch survey.

It's even been the subject of spoofs by other products (like Hamlet) and TV comedy sketch shows. A Dave Allen sketch from the mid-seventies showed a puppy wrapped in toilet roll running down the stairs followed by a furious Allen with his trousers around his ankles.

18 SHAKE'N'VAC
DANCING WOMAN 1979

As with toilet paper, your average house-hold cleaning product can be difficult to sell. They're not sexy, they won't get you the boy or girl of your dreams, and they won't make you the envy of your fellow human beings. How strange, then, that an ad for a powdery carpet cleaner should rank as one of the most remembered commercials of all time. Perhaps it's because the Shake'N'Vac ad made us all think that cleaning the front room carpet *could* actually change our lives in some way. After all, 'it's all you have to do,' according to the dancing woman in the ad.

Before Shake'N'Vac came along, Jenny Logan was a stage actress who had appeared in many West End musicals. During one production of *Chicago*, Logan was spotted by an ad director who was casting for a commercial which features a housewife singing her way through her daily duties. Logan had done plenty of ads, but her day's filming at a studio in Notting Hill was to earn her a place in British advertising history. The shoot, however, was less than enjoyable. 'I remember as I was being made up that I had this overwhelming nausea come over me and I was sick for most of the day,' she recalls. 'Every time I went off set I was being ill. I was not very well at all. If I look a bit manic in the advert, that was why...leaping about up and down didn't make me feel any better.' In the ad, Logan's character tries to rid her living room of stale smells (demonstrated by a vanishing pet dog and a smoking ashtray) by shaking a tube of Shake'N'Vac on the carpet and then vacuuming it up. But it was no ordinary 'shake'. Aided by a choreographer, Logan was required to shuffle in a backward motion while sprinkling the white powder in a zigzag fashion. 'If you just shake it backwards and forwards it doesn't work. You have to go up and down as well. You have to do the dance otherwise you don't get the powder out the right way,' says Logan.

The actress also had to sing the rock'n'roll theme tune which went: 'Do the Shake'N'Vac, and put the freshness back.' The soon-to-be famous ad, glorious in its British suburban naffness, ran for over ten years, during which time Logan became known throughout the UK as the 'The Shake'N'Vac woman'. Logan was once invited on to a daytime TV show to perform the song in front of a studio audience who (to her surprise) knew the words better than she did. It comes as no surprise that, at one point, Logan went into the recording studio to put her magnum opus down on tape. 'It was supposed to be similar to the *Birdy Song* – they were going to play it all over the Costa Del Sol,' she recalls.

The song was rather disturbingly renamed *Do The Shake Attack,* but sadly (or perhaps not) the record never saw the light of day. For all its perceived naffness and ability to make people laugh, the Shake'N'Vac ad achieved what it set out to achieve – it sold a product that few people had heard of beforehand, leaving ad man Trevor Beattie one of its biggest fans. 'It's slagged off by the business and people saying: "Oh, it's so bad it's good"...but name me two other famous carpet cleaners? It's fantastic branding. You call it "The Shake'N'Vac ad" – you don't call it "That ad where the woman goes round with the powdery stuff".'

'The worst commercial on television,' as it was once labelled, is said to have brought the product a 60 per cent share of a market worth around £9 million a year. Who's laughing now? Not surprisingly, Shake'N'Vac *did* change Jenny Logan's life – if in an unexpected way. Suddenly, her career in TV ads was over. 'I couldn't make another one because after that I was so recognisable in the advert world. They [advertisers] didn't want me associated with another product,' she says.

17 CARLING BLACK LABEL
DAMBUSTERS 1989

Carling Black Label has provided us with some of the funniest ads in British advertising history. Like Heineken and Double Diamond before it, the premise is simple – drink this lager and all your problems will disappear, and any feat will be achievable. In fact, short of turning you into Superman, there seems nothing that a pint of Carling Black Label can't do. Even saving a bouncing bomb is now possible. Back at the turn of the seventies Carling Black Label was outselling all other lagers. But a decade later sales were starting to dip. Carling was perceived as a beer for older drinkers when the ad agency WCRS came up with a new idea to appeal to younger customers. The agency wanted to use eighties wit and irreverence to appeal to young drinkers; they needed a campaign that would make Carling's drinkers think they were just a little bit cleverer than anyone else.

Their new campaign was full of fun and British humour. It included a spoof on the Old Spice ad, with a surfer sailing in through the pub door and up to the bar on the back of an enormous wave; and a memorable spot showing a window cleaner wiping the windows on the outside of a plane – while it's airborne! 'I bet he drinks Carling Black Label,' was the famous observation. 'Nah, he's missed a bit,' came the reply. Incidentally, Nick Kamen's famous Levi's Launderette ad was also turned on its head by Carling, but the first person of whom the famous 'I bet' observation could be made was the rather less sexy snooker referee Len Ganley, who had just crushed a snooker ball in his white glove.

But perhaps the greatest Carling ad of the lot was an imaginative, 60-second spoof of the World War Two epic movie, *The Dambusters*. The ad was directed by Roger Woodburn, who had shot the Carling 'Surfer' and 'Launderette' ad as well as the last ever 'Heineken Refreshes' spot about supermarket trolleys returning home. Ironically, the director admits he doesn't drink beer himself. Woodburn was a former modelmaker for Gerry 'Thunderbirds' Anderson and had also been a special effects supervisor; they were skills that were to come in handy for this ad. The 'Dambusters' commercial featured two British comedians (Stephen Frost and Mark Arden, who had appeared in many of the new Carling ads) as pilots unloading bouncing bombs on a German dam being patrolled by a soldier on night duty.

As the bombs bounce along the water towards the precious dam the German soldier turns goalkeeper, diving left and right to deflect and catch the British missiles. Woodburn and his team had considered using the actual footage from the film *The Dam Busters* but the royalties proved prohibitive – so they re-created the scene themselves on a lake in Scotland. Meanwhile, the cockpit came courtesy

of a World War Two enthusiast who had kept it in his back garden. However, the actual 'bomb' in the shots was only a tennis ball, propelled by a tennis machine, and bouncing on salt in a studio! Finally, the 'German goalkeeping' scene was shot in Pinewood Studios. The dam wall was built from polystyrene, but the stone slabs around it were made out of rubber as the actor kept crashing into them while diving for the ball.

Fortunately for Woodburn the air date for the ad was a long way off – so he had plenty of time to experiment and to get it right. And got it right he did. Even though the ad makers cleared the idea with the Dambusters Squadron, complaints that it was in bad taste inevitably poured in. But lager drinkers loved it – sales of Carling Black Label grew by 10 per cent in the first two years that the ad was on the air. It proved as popular an ad in Britain's cinemas as it was a welcome break on TV.

16 COKE
TEACH THE WORLD TO SING **1971**

It's the real thing. Coke.

It has been called 'one of the most defining ads of the century'. And when copywriter Bill Backer's plane landed in fog in Ireland one night in 1971, little did he realise that the incident would lead to a commercial that would change the face of advertising. Backer, who worked for the American company McCann Erickson, was forced to stay overnight in an airport departures lounge, where he witnessed a group of passengers forgetting their differences by sharing cans of Coca Cola. The copywriter scribbled the idea down on an airport serviette and an idea, if not his plane, was about to take off. That summer, the ad makers gathered together on an Italian hilltop young people who were working at the country's foreign embassies. (The original plan had been to film it in the English countryside but the shoot was rained off.) And so to sunnier Rome where, miming to the words of The New Seekers, 30 young people of different races and religions – and all dressed in national costume – were seen uniting around a bottle of Coke. It was to be one of the first occasions where non-white faces had been seen (in a positive light anyway) in a British TV ad.

However, the star of the ad, who featured in the opening shot – wasn't from India, Italy or Israel. She was an English teenager called Linda Higson – a nanny in Rome – who was seen singing those now famous opening words: 'I'd like to buy the world a home and furnish it with love.' 'I was sitting in a café in Rome one day, just around the corner from where I lived, and some people came up to me and asked me if I'd be interested in starring in an advert. They'd already started – but they just needed a face to start off the whole thing,' recalls Higson, now Linda Neary. 'I had no idea what it was about until a week later when I had to go to a hotel and learn a song. I can hardly sing a note! There was no mention of singing. If they'd have mentioned singing, you wouldn't have seen me for dust. Our family are not known for their musical ability.' But Neary never made it to that Italian hilltop with all the other young folk. Her part was filmed separately, at the Rome Pony Club. It was only by a trick of editing that it seemed that Neary was standing among them. 'I had no concept of what the rest of the advert was like. I didn't even know there was a huge crowd scene. It was just a day of work really, for some extra cash to go travelling,' she recalls. Neary may have only made £150 from the ad (even though her face ended up being seen around the world and even on beermats!) but the money did enable her to quit her job and see the world. However, the ad *was* an expensive shoot, costing over $200,000. The money would turn out to be well spent.

The 60-second spot had a universal appeal through its 'peace' theme in difficult times, which made it as relevant in Egypt as it was in England. It was in tune with the youth of the day – anti-war, anti-capitalist and pro-community; it seemed all the nations of the world belonged to one big, happy family.

When Linda Neary returned home from her travels after her nannying stint in Rome, she returned to Cheshire as a world famous TV star. 'I went travelling for six months with a girlfriend. We went off to Greece and Turkey and travelled round Europe,' she recalls. 'When I arrived back in England, it [the ad] had really taken off over here and my face was known all over the place. It was a very strange kind of sensation.' These days we take it for granted that some of the ads we see in the UK are also being seen by TV viewers in other countries thousands of miles away. But prior to this ad, that wasn't the case; Coke helped make TV advertising global (although most of the ads we see in this country are still intended for Britain only). Not all the countries of the world, however, were delighted to show the ad. It was reported that South Africa, in the throes of apartheid, requested a version which didn't feature black people. The ad agency refused to grant the request.

Two Top 40 hits resulted from the ad – one for The New Seekers (re-recorded without the product name) and another for the appropriately named Hillside Singers, selling over a million copies between them. The song was co-written by Roger Greenaway, who was responsible for other classic jingles such as 'If you like a lot of chocolate on your biscuit join our club' for Jacob's Club and 'Jeans On' for Brutus Jeans. The theme of the famous 1971 ad, which ran for six years, was to be revisited by Coca Cola several times over the decades. Christmas versions showed new sets of singers on a hilltop holding candles, while in 1990 the original cast members, including Linda Neary, were reunited with their children in tow for a nostalgic follow-up which continued the theme of global harmony.

15 NIKE
PARK LIFE **1997**

Jonathan Glazer is one of Britain's most talented young ad directors. As well as shooting memorable pop promos, like Jamiroquai's *Virtual Insanity*, he has also made some of the most talked-about ads of the nineties. And yet, if we believe the ad agency creatives who came up with the idea for this Nike ad, one of Glazer's main qualifications for directing the ad was that he played Sunday League football, so knew the subject matter well! Nike (the Goddess of Victory in Greek mythology) was founded in 1971. In the eighties its 'Just Do It' campaign threw up one of the most popular advertising slogans of the time. Famous sportsmen like basketball's Michael Jordan were the public faces of its sports products. In the late nineties, Nike felt it had achieved high credibility in certain sports like basketball and athletics, but football was not one of them – sportswear firms like Umbro and Adidas were ahead in that particular game. The aim of this campaign was to change that perception.

The ad starts with a wife bemoaning her husband's infatuation with the game as we see a Sunday morning egg being cracked into a frying pan. 'Shut up,' comes the admonishing voice (that of Brian Clough), and suddenly we are on the football pitch, with Blur's *Park Life* blasting away in accompaniment. Filmed on Hackney Marshes (its 74 pitches make it the biggest football park of its kind in Europe), the ad agency managed to gather together four of the English Premier League's most popular footballers – Eric Cantona, Ian Wright, Robbie Fowler and David Seaman – and film them as if they were taking part in an ordinary Sunday League game. Nearly 250 players from many different leagues took part, including women teams, a Nigerian eleven and an Asian side. The amateur players were only told they were turning up to take part in a Nike ad – they had no idea that the likes of Eric 'Ooh Aah' Cantona would be there too. Glazer recalls that the scenes involving each star were filmed on a separate day – Cantona on day one (dressed in a pub team's number 11 shirt), Fowler day two, Seaman on day three and Ian Wright on day four. 'I think Ian Wright got the most affection [from the amateur players],' recalls Glazer.

'Cantona...they had this kind of weird respectful distance from – they gave him a wide berth wherever he walked.' Some shots (like Seaman palming the ball over the bar) were deliberately set up by Glazer – while other images used in the final ad came from five-minute matches which the teams would play. Trying to keep the shoot secret soon proved an impossibility. Each day schoolchildren from all over the local area would turn up in their lunch hour to see some of the biggest names in English football having a kick around – mainly with a lot of out-of-condition blokes from local pub teams. 'That was the extraordinary thing about the idea,' says Glazer. 'These guys would go home that night and say: "I played with Ian Wright today" or "I passed the ball to Eric Cantona".'

14 BT
'OLOGY' **1988**

British Telecom has a record of plumping for individual characters to represent the company – from Buzby the Bird to Bob 'It's Good To Talk' Hoskins – and more recently ET the alien, who was promoting the notion of 'phoning home' in an earlier stage of its career. But the series of ads featuring comic actress Maureen Lipman topped the lot in terms of popularity. It felt like comedy straight out of a BBC sitcom – and it was a triumph of good judgement over market research.

Lipman was born in Hull in 1946. Before signing up with BT she'd had a successful acting career in TV sitcoms and dramas like *Agony* and *Cold Enough For Snow*. She'd also been the star of a successful stage show about the life of Joyce Grenfell. And yet, after all that hard work, a series of classic ads was to rocket her into everyone's front room. By the late eighties, everyone knew who Maureen Lipman was. The series of 'Beattie' ads was devised by Richard Phillips of ad agency J Walter Thompson. The previous BT ads had featured various furry animals – but all were about to become extinct; the client wanted a fresh, new campaign.

Phillips' brief from BT was 'to encourage people to understand the value of a phone call in an inter-family relationship, i.e. phone your mother'. The copywriter believed he had at last found a job that was perfect for him – 'a nice Jewish boy of nearly 40 years experience being asked to write a commercial about phoning your mother!' he later recalled. Phillips immediately wrote a script in which a Jewish mother complained about her son never calling and then, when he did call, complaining that he only called and never visited! But British Telecom wanted a campaign of four ads – Phillips was forced to come up with three more ideas – one was to feature the mother (initially named 'Dora') shopping; another had her delivering a birthday greeting by phone; and the last was to meet the brief for an ad on a 'Congratulations' theme. (This was to become the celebrated 'ology' commercial.) Phillips still had two hurdles to overcome – his fears that Jews would be offended, and further worries that non-Jews wouldn't find the ads funny. He carried out personal research which overcame his concerns, but research by BT wasn't quite so positive. In fact, it was downright damnatory. Fortunately for Phillips and the ad agency BT managers chose to ignore the findings of their own market research.

Despite being 30 years younger than the woman she was being asked to play, Maureen Lipman took on the role and filmed a series of ten BT commercials, directed by Tony Smith, who made the BBC series *Tutti Frutti*. Before transmission, the ads were once more put out to market research – and the results were equally

negative. Again, BT bosses ignored the researcher's advice and went with their instincts. In 1988 the 'Beattie' campaign (her name had been changed thanks to a suggestion by Lipman) hit the airwaves. It was an immediate success. Soon Beattie had a ready-made husband (Harry), a son called Melvyn and grandchildren called Anthony, Oliver and Natalie. Richard Wilson, Clive Swift and Caroline Quentin were among the team of actors that co-starred with Lipman in the ads. There was also a catchphrase – or rather a 'catchword' – 'Ology' as in the line 'An Ology. He gets an ology and he says he's failed. You get an ology you're a scientist'. (Beattie had said it to her under-performing schoolboy grandson.)

Soon the character had entered the national psyche – aided by '20 Things You Didn't Know About Your Favourite Jewish Momma' in *The Sun*. Just over a year later Richard Phillips had completed his 26th Beattie ad featuring Maureen Lipman and was writing a book on the advertising campaign. Lipman was left philosophising on the fact that it had taken her 22 years to become a household name – 'like Harpic' she mused. And meanwhile, back in Hull, Maureen Lipman's mother (who had been quoted in the press saying she preferred Mercury because it was cheaper) was being asked to open local telephone shops.

13 YELLOW PAGES
J.R. HARTLEY **1983**

'My name? Yes, it's J...R... Hartley.' The subject of child stars in ads has been well documented. Patsy Kensit was the Birds Eye Peas girl; Leslie Ash asked mummy why her hands were so soft; and Jonathan Ross snap, crackle and popped his way through a Rice Krispies ad. This campaign for Yellow Pages goes to the other end of the scale – featuring an actor who didn't achieve stardom until his seventies. The big, yellow services directory (with the famous index entry 'Boring – see civil engineers') had been the subject of well-known campaigns before. 'Let your fingers do the walking' had entered the lingo back in 1974 and ran (not walked) for a decade. But by the early eighties research was showing that people associated Yellow Pages with the nastier things in life, such as emergency plumbing.

The advertising agency Abbot Mead Vickers was brought in to change that perception and to help give the directory a more positive image. Writer David Abbott and art director Ron Brown came up with an idea that would feature an elderly man using Yellow Pages to help him search for rare book on British butterflies. However, they thought the subject matter a little obscure and changed it to fly-fishing.

All they had to do was to cast the man to play its fictional author, J.R. Hartley. Norman Lumsden was a former commercial artist for the Ministry of Transport, who had turned to acting and singing – taking part in countless televised operas and TV series, where he usually played the butler. (He'd also appeared in dozens of British and American commercials.) But after decade upon decade attending casting sessions Lumsden was to arrive, already well past retirement age, at a session for a part that was to change his life. 'When I got there I found about 12 other old boys, all different. Some with hair and some without, some fat and some thin,' Lumsden recalls. 'We were all given a script and some of the chaps weren't taking their work too seriously, and were too busy talking about their past experiences...but I was busy beavering away.'

Lumsden got the job. He was required to play the part of a retired author (so the end of the ad reveals) who was looking for a copy of *Fly Fishing* – a book he'd obviously written many decades earlier. Hartley is seen traipsing round second-hand bookshops in London in search of the elusive book, eventually finding it in far less exhaustive circumstances – by ringing round places he's found in the Yellow Pages. The ad was directed by Bob 'Smash Martians' Brooks – and within a few weeks of it being shown, Lumsden found the sort of fame that had eluded him all his career. 'I just took it for granted – it was something good that had clicked,' says Lumsden.

As one of the newspapers said at the time: 'J.R. Hartley's biggest catch has been the public imagination.' As for the appeal of the ad (which went on to run for 12 years) Lumsden has his own theory. 'So much advertising these days is "punch, punch, punch" – noise and loud music that's unnecessary. J.R. Hartley always came across as a lovely quiet pause in it all.' Lumsden went on to film several more ads for Yellow Pages, including one where he took up the game of golf (Lumsden's own favourite pastime), but none surpassed the charming appeal of the first. In 1991, in a strange case of fiction becoming fact, a book called *Fly Fishing* by J.R. Hartley was written (by real life author Michael Russell) and went to the top of the Christmas bestseller list. To confuse matters further, the fictional character Hartley was seen signing his 'own' book in another ad for Yellow Pages. Years after the campaign ended Norman Lumsden feels that the fictional author is still a big part of his own life. 'I think of him as a friend – a very dear friend. I even feel he's taken me over. Honestly, I feel more J.R. Hartley these days than I do Norman Lumsden.'

12 RENAULT CLIO
PAPA ET NICOLE **1991**

There seems to be an unwritten rule that we Brits can put up with foreigners in our ads as long as we find them faintly amusing. Victor Kiam, the Italian Ambassador, Papa and Nicole...they all fit into what psychologist Dr David Lewis sees as an 'underlying xenophobia that one finds in this culture. Foreigners can be presented on screen provided they match up to the stereotypical image we have of that particular country,' he says. 'Everyone in this country knows that French people are hopelessly romantic, amazingly sexy, fantastically virile and potent. All the girls are beautiful and all the men are handsome.' And so, leaving aside questions about how the Hunchback of Nôtre Dame might fit into all this, we have the immensely popular 'Papa/Nicole' campaign for Renault – which does indeed fit in with all our preconceptions of our French cousins.

As the hopeful successor to the Renault Five, the Renault Clio was launched on the British market in 1991, in competition with makes like the Ford Fiesta and Vauxhall Nova. Renault's fortunes were at an all-time low. All that was to change with a campaign featuring characters who had to reflect the car's 'personality' – the small car with big-car refinement. It was a campaign that ran for five years. The new series of Renault ads was also designed so that nearly all potential buyers of the car would identify with someone in the stories – young females with Nicole, men and older people with Papa. Even if they didn't directly identify with one of the characters, everyone could aspire to the relaxed, Provencal lifestyle which, despite our historical anti-Frenchness, was sure to be an attractive proposition.

The first Papa/Nicole ad was launched on April Fools Day 1991. It showed Papa (played by French poet Max Douchin) lend the keys of his Clio to daughter Nicole (Estelle Skornik, who couldn't, in real life, drive!). She then went off on a romantic assignation while Papa (as befits our view of all French men) trundled off on a similar, secret liaison. Then father and daughter reunite, unaware of each other's movements. They greet with a minimalist exchange that wouldn't have tested many actors: Papa: 'Nicole?' Nicole: 'Papa?'

There was something about these attractive, sophisticated, well-to-do people enjoying life to the full that appealed to British viewers. Market research revealed that people saw the new Renault Clio as being one of the 'smarter' small cars, one that well-to-do people would drive. After initial success inspired by the ad, Renault found that other small cars – like the Peugeot 106 and the Nissan Micra – were snatching back their share of the market.

The Papa/Nicole saga had no option but to continue the work it had begun. The ongoing storyline helped increase sales and its share of the market each year throughout the early nineties. In 1992, Nicole was seen in her finest dress for a night out – taking the Clio while Papa was forced to go out on her boyfriend's motorbike. In 1993, Papa and Nicole were seen on a family holiday in the French Alps; in 1994 Nicole is transformed from a pretty young girl into a sophisticated young woman; and in 1995 Nicole's grandmother pays a surprise visit.

Three years later this much-loved series came to an end when (in a bizarre but inspired piece of casting that made the campaign feel it belonged to us Brits) Nicole ditched comedian Vic Reeves at the altar – and drove off into the sunset with his comedy partner Bob Mortimer. It was estimated that 23 million people tuned in to see a denouement which Renault called: 'The wedding of the year – but to whom?' in press releases. Quite what psychologists would make of the glamorous heroine making a quick getaway with a former solicitor from Middlesbrough is anyone's guess. Writer Fay Weldon was certainly bemused. 'I don't see how anyone would make a romantic getaway in a Renault Clio – too small!'

11 **CINZANO BIANCO**
COLLINS AND ROSSITER **1978**

What we TV viewers don't see, we don't tend to miss. But it's interesting to muse on what might have been. The original scripts for the now famous Cinzano Bianco ads featured Sean Connery and Woody Allen – but neither, unsurprisingly, were available. The original idea behind the campaign was to spoof the Martini ads and their 'beautiful people', right down to filming with hot air balloons. But when director Alan Parker got involved, the concept was dragged back into a much simpler form, centred around the comedy skills of actor Leonard Rossiter. Rossiter was the star of the hit ITV sitcom (and how infrequently those three words would pop up together in television history) *Rising Damp,* which ran from 1974 to 1978.

Playing the seedy landlord Rigsby, Rossiter became one of the most popular comedy actors in Britain – so was perfect for an ad campaign which would sell a product through humour. Parker recalls going to see Rossiter at his London home when the idea of the Cinzano Bianco campaign came up. 'We kind of agreed that, actually, the script was absolute rubbish. So Leonard said: "What I'd like to do is the old music hall joke."' He picked up his cup of tea that was sitting there in his living room, looked at his watch and turned the cup and he said: "You know – that joke." So we said: "Yeah, that's a very good joke, particularly if it happened to be Joan Collins that you were spilling it on."'

Out of one idea over a cup of tea one of Britain's most popular advertising campaigns was born. Collins, who had just finished filming *The Stud,* was soon signed up and Parker began filming with scripts from Collett Dickenson Pearce writer Ron Collins. The first ad showed Rossiter and Collins sitting next to each other on an international flight. Rossiter accidentally presses a pad on Collins' chair which projects her backwards, her Cinzano Bianco and ice spilling down her cleavage. 'Getting your head down, sweetie?' asks Rossiter (in a line he added himself). The 'spilling gag' was to become the central feature in each of the following ads.

Terry Lovelock, who had come up with the 'Heineken Refreshes the Parts' slogan a few years earlier, wrote and directed two later ads with Collins and Rossiter. They included one where Collins gets drenched with Cinzano Bianco, thanks to some Japanese businessman who thinks throwing the drink at her is some sort of British tradition (which it was, in these ads anyway). 'Joan was thoroughly professional and got the idea straight away. She was very, very self-protective, very intelligent and absolutely unpretentious,' says Lovelock. 'Leonard Rossiter... from the theatre... difficult. He felt he was "the main man" – he was the artist of the two and he would choreograph himself. His relationship with her [Collins] was one of great respect between them – they worked together wonderfully well and this was a successful campaign, but he used to refer to her as "the prop"!' But even though the public loved the ads, there was debate in the industry as to whether they actually worked. It was reported that some people seemed to think they

were for Martini, the tipple that the ad makers had originally set out to spoof! Whether it was for this reason or any other (some say the company wanted to run a global campaign that couldn't rely on funny scripts in one language) the comedy partnership was terminated after five years.

Collins was to reinvent herself as Alexis in the American series *Dynasty* while Rossiter carried on making *The Fall and Rise of Reginald Perrin*. He died in 1984, aged 57 – a sad loss to British comedy.

Over 20 years later Parker explains that the Cinzano Bianco ads were filmed with the same ethos as other Collet Dickenson Pearce ads. This was to 'not talk down to the audience, to use humour, and to be honest about the product...and therefore if someone is interested in what you are doing – and what you are doing is interesting – somebody might buy it'. He continues: 'It worked – boy did it work. There was a period of time when the commercials were by far and away the most interesting thing you could see that evening on television. They were infinitely more entertaining than the programmes were in those days.'

10 IMPULSE
CHANCE ENCOUNTER **1998**

It took British advertising nearly two decades to portray black people in a positive light – the Coke 'I'd Like To Teach The World To Sing' ad was the first time many TV viewers had seen non-whites in a commercial. But that was in 1971. It was to be another three decades before the advertisers decided the public wouldn't be offended by an ad with a gay story line. Up until 'Chance Encounter', ads for Impulse body spray had been pretty conventional – a man is mesmerised by the scent of a passing woman and, with great haste, buys flowers from a market stall and runs after her. 'Men just can't help acting on Impulse,' was the slogan. And women were supposed to go out and buy the stuff off the back of it.

But on May 18th 1998 the men featured in the latest Impulse ad were more likely to be acting on impulse with each other than they were with the women in the commercial. Set to the tune of *'The Female of the Species'* by Space, we see a young woman dropping her possessions after bumping into a hunk of a man. As he bends down to help her pick them up, their eyes – and hands – meet and they exchange a smile we know so well from ads like these. But then the unexpected happens – the man is whisked away by another man. It quickly dawns on the woman that she is walking through a gay part of the city.

We know this because a few gay symbols are helpfully thrown in – like a small dog dressed in leather, not to mention the writer Quentin Crisp who flew in from New York for a two-second part in the ad.

Ad agency Ogilvy and Mather (which had previously written a never-shown 'gay ad' for Guinness) reckons that in the week leading up to the commercial being aired it received almost half a million pounds worth of free publicity due to coverage in the press. 'Now even gay men are acting on Impulse'; 'Boy meets girl but leaves with boy as scent of change blows through TV'; and 'Ad to be gay – body spray breaks last TV taboo' were among the headlines written in the British press. Apparently much research into the probable response from the gay community took place before the ad was shown. The research concluded that Impulse was presenting a positive image of gay men – precisely, it concluded, because they can be so easily mistaken for straight men. And although some men may have been offended by the ad, Ogilvy and Mather reckoned that Impulse buyers – mainly teenage girls – would be hip and forward-thinking enough to get the joke.

It was a case of advertising being behind the times – 'being gay' might have been taboo in advertising terms, but it certainly wasn't as far as the target audience was concerned. However, being an ad which would still no doubt split opinion to some

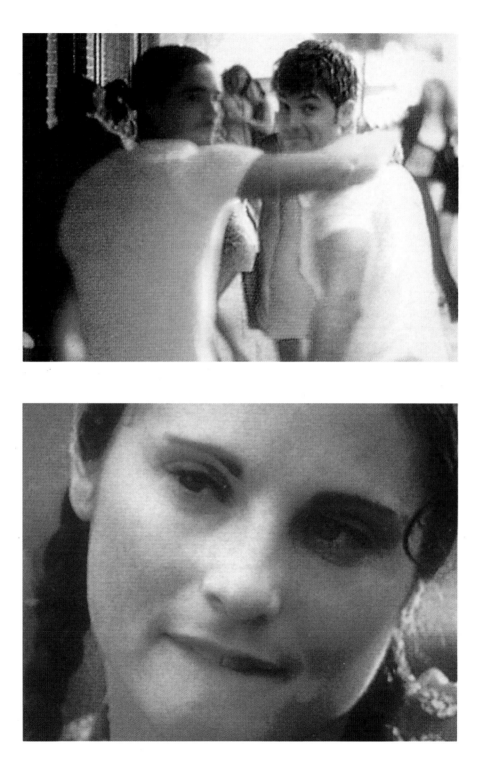

extent by addressing homosexuality, it could only be shown after 7.30pm. Adam Mattera, editor of *Attitude* magazine, concludes that the ad came out at just the right time for Impulse. 'At the time the ad came out I think there was a real feeling in society that "gay" was more acceptable – it was more mainstream and just on the cusp of TV shows like *Queer As Folk,*' says Mattera. 'I think Impulse really anticipated that trend and went with it. They [the men in the ad] were very normal, they weren't drag queens or covered in leather or anything – they were just like regular guys walking down the street. It just rode on the crest of that whole sort of zeitgeist at the time.'

However, as brave as the Impulse ad was, the jury is still out (even if the characters in ads, on the whole, aren't) on whether it can really be called 'groundbreaking' or even 'trendsetting'. Was the ad really showing a positive image of gay men? Or were we merely being invited to sympathise with a straight woman who had wandered into a gay ghetto? Whatever, it was a start. And despite openly gay personalities like Graham Norton now being able to front TV advertising campaigns we're still unlikely to see many gay scenarios in a TV ad – not unless it's one of those ridiculous late-night ones for chatlines.

9 WALKERS CRISPS
GARY LINEKER 1993

Gary Lineker was one of *the* British footballing heroes of the eighties and nineties – that now rare breed of clean-living, good-tempered, happily-married centre forward, who also happened to be the top scorer in the 1990 World Cup finals in Italy. After a distinguished career with Leicester City, Everton, Tottenham Hotspur and Barcelona, Lineker spent the last year of his playing career in Japan playing for a team called Grampus Eight. Meanwhile, back in England, just as Lineker was putting on his boots for the last time, ad supremo John Webster was looking at a new campaign for Walkers Crisps.

After years in hooligan-induced doldrums, English football was now beginning to find its feet with Sky Sports and the Premier League; it was time for football to form an unbeatable team with advertising and sell, sell, sell.

Walkers began life as a small company in Leicester (Lineker's home town) that had prospered and been taken over by a big American company that required a big campaign with impact. It was suggested that Webster might be interested in using the homecoming Lineker in a Walkers ad; after all, his Uncle Ken had been a greengrocer in Leicester and had supplied Walkers with potatoes. Lineker seemed the perfect choice.

All that was needed now was an entertaining way of using him. John Webster had an idea. 'He was known as Mr Nice Guy because he's never been booked in all his career,' he explains. 'We thought it would be interesting to turn him into a nasty guy who pinched crisps. Gary saw the joke and went ahead with it. The campaign was born.' There was, however, one small problem; unlike Gary, the Americans didn't see the joke. Recalls Webster: 'They said: "You can't have an English sporting hero being a thief – come on!" We said: "Everyone will know it's a joke." They tried to force us to shoot an ending where Lineker gives the crisps back to the kid – but we ignored that.' The ad showed Lineker returning to his home city, kissing babies and waving at passers-by who recognise the local hero, as *Welcome Home* by Peters and Lee plays in the background. When Lineker comes across a boy eating a packet of Walkers Crisps, his Mr Nice Guy image deserts him and he runs off into the distance with the distraught boy's snack.

Lineker recalls that not everyone was impressed while he was shooting the ad in 1993, just after his return from Japan. 'I was outside Leicester train station shooting a bit with a newspaper vendor and there were a lot of people watching in the town centre. A little lady comes up to me and she taps me on the shoulder and says: "Are you Gary Lineker?" I say: "Yeah, that's right." She says: "I thought so.

What's going on here then, are they expecting anybody special?'"

After filming an initial four ads in the first year of the campaign, Lineker soon signed up to film more. The campaign caught the public's imagination. His follow-ups included ads with the Spice Girls and his former England team mate Paul Gascoigne, who was pictured in tears after Lineker crushed his fingers in his Walkers crisps packet – it is Lineker's own favourite ad. Seven years on Lineker has now shot over 30 ads for Walkers and the campaign is as successful as ever. The value of annual sales of Walkers Crisps in the UK is now £420 million – three times more than that of its nearest competitor in the snack market – and Webster's campaign has played no small part in bringing about that success.

As well as starring in ads for popular snacks Gary Lineker has carved out another career for himself since returning from Japan – that of television personality. He is a captain in the panel quiz *They Think It's All Over* and presenter of *Match of The Day*. The fact that the Walkers ads have let us see Lineker in a new light – one of humorous self-depreciation – can't have hindered the progression of his television career. After all, here's a footballer that can walk, talk and take the mickey out of himself at the same time. Move over, Des Lynam.

Paul Weiland, who has directed most of Lineker's ads, admits to having been impressed by his acting talents. 'He's as good as any actor that I work with now,' says Weiland, who directed the TV series *Mr Bean* as well as several other ads in this Top 100. 'He knows exactly what to do. He knows how to hold the crisp perfectly. And he won't ever be caught with a packet of Golden Wonder – you know that about Gary.' The last word goes to John Webster, who helped bring the 'No More Mr Nice Guy' campaign to our screens: 'They [the American owners of Walkers] still can't understand how we did it and how English people don't go against him because he pinches kids' crisps. The English sense of humour is strange, isn't it?'

8 HAMLET
HAPPINESS IS... **1964**

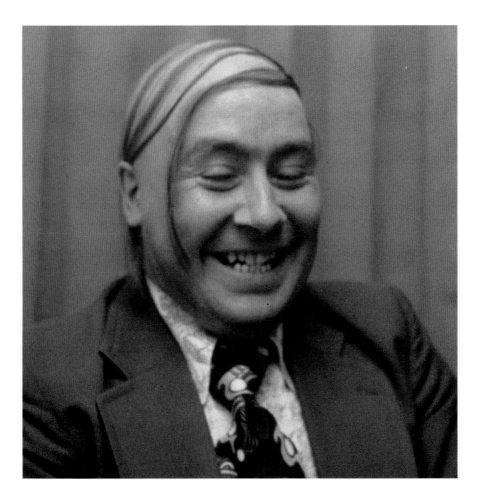

William Shakespeare would need a relaxing puff on a cigar if he knew that probably more British people now associate the name 'Hamlet' with tobacco than with his famous play. The blame goes to Collett Dickinson Pearce (CDP) copywriter Tim Warriner and art director Roy Carruthers who were on the bus home one rainy night in 1963, while in search of inspiration for a new campaign for a cigar called Hamlet. Warriner had been having problems lighting his cigarette in the rain. As the bus made its way through the misty streets of London the pair looked out of the window and saw a Charles Schultz 'Peanuts' poster, with a picture of Snoopy and the phrase: 'Happiness Is...'. At last, Warriner managed to light up a cigarette. He leaned back into his bus seat and exclaimed: 'Happiness is a dry cigarette on the number 34 bus.' And then came the idea to incorporate it into his latest project.

A year later the campaign was launched featuring a man in bed with a broken leg in plaster, and who only finds happiness by lighting up a Hamlet cigar. Setting a pattern for the next 40 years, the only words were the bus journey-inspired slogan at the end of the ad (voiced by actor John Carson) followed by: 'The mild cigar from Benson and Hedges.' Groundbreaking too was its use of music to help give a product personality. Soon, everybody knew the melody of Bach's *Air On A G String,* even if the vast majority only knew it as 'the tune from Hamlet'. This was one of the first ad campaigns to attract viewers' attention through its gently enjoyable humour.

Film director Alan Parker was one of the early directors on the Hamlet campaign, at a time, he believes, when making TV ads was one of the most creative jobs going. Opportunities in TV programme-making were few and far between then, and the British film industry was in a depressed state. Ad campaigns like Hamlet provided young directors like Parker, Ridley Scott and Hugh Hudson with a chance to express themselves. 'I think Hamlet was the first of a breed of commercials that start from the basis of something that's problematic, to which the product offers happiness and the solution,' says Parker. 'That became a very famous construction that was pinched and borrowed by many other products, including Heineken.'

Parker enjoyed the challenge of the early ads with only its brief mention of the product at the end of the ad – something typical at that time of campaigns by the ad agency Collett Dickenson Pearce. Over the years Hamlet ads would take on a familiar format. They'd begin with a mini-disaster or embarrassment – like a golfer who couldn't get his ball out of the bunker or a bald man whose wig is knocked off in a restaurant – and then offer a solution. In other words, the cigars would come out and get lit up, and as the first puff of smoke hit the air that now familiar theme tune would strike up to accompany a happy (or at least, peaceful) ending. The message was simple: a Hamlet cigar might not make you lead a trouble-free life, but it will help you deal with life's little traumas. Or so smokers thought anyway – with the result that Hamlet has accounted for half the cigars sold in Britain for much of the last 40 years.

Paul Weiland, who directed Hamlet ads in the seventies (such as the golfer in the bunker), believes the secret of the campaign was its simplicity – and situations that everyone could relate to. 'It was this thing of – when something goes wrong, *this* was satisfaction. *This* would get you over the hump. The best campaign ideas in advertising are when it's very simple and you can borrow from any area –

whether film, theatre, real life or press.' Indeed, CDP was quick to take advantage of the latest trends and news stories. One ad was rushed out in just a few days following the collapse of the stock market. The Hamlet campaign is one of actor (and ad maker) Griff Rhys Jones' favourites in British TV advertising. 'The strength of a good campaign is that it has legs. It goes somewhere and you can find other variations on it,' says Rhys Jones. 'The Hamlet campaign is brilliant. It's a very, very, very simple idea. But it just takes that idea and says: "This is our idea and we'll have that. Anybody that does anything similar to that is going to be in Hamlet territory. The music comes up and you can instantly recognise it. Fantastic."'

Perhaps the best loved of all Hamlet ads featured Scottish comedy actor Gregor Fisher in 1987. Fisher had played a character known as 'The Baldy Man' in the BBC2 sketch show *Naked Video*. One of his sketches was turned into an ad featuring the man attempting to get his picture taken in a photo booth, while doing his best to cover his all but bald pate. Just as each flash appears The Baldy Man suffers a setback – his thin but long strands of hair fall over his face, he is caught bending forward to see if the machine is working, and finally his seat collapses. It was a classic piece of perfectly executed silent comedy that was cheap to make and left viewers in no doubt as to which product it was advertising. (It was voted best ad in the world at Cannes in the mid-nineties.) But all good things must come to an end and one of the greatest campaigns in advertising history did just that in 1999, after over a hundred commercials. The Government introduced legislation that decreed that cigar advertising would follow cigarette ads into the ashtray of TV advertising history. Suddenly, Hamlet's TV campaign was no more. Cue rising puff of cigar smoke and cue, for the last time, *that* music.

7 R WHITES LEMONADE
SECRET LEMONADE DRINKER **1973**

Perhaps the biggest surprise in *The 100 Greatest TV Ads* was the appearance of this cult campaign in the Top Ten – a tale of two Elvis's. There was no block voting from R Whites' employees, copywriters at ad agency Allen Brady Marsh (who created it) or even fans of a certain English pop star; apparently, this campaign simply touched a nerve with people of a certain age – people like broadcaster Stuart Maconie for instance. 'Even as a kid I always used to like the idea of R Whites Lemonade because it seemed so non-corporate compared to Coca Cola or MacDonalds, which were these huge multinationals,' Maconie reminisces. 'I never knew where R Whites Lemonade had come from. Who was R White? The name always used to conjure up this idea of a bloke in a shed distilling it while his wife would say: "Come in now, our White, your tea's ready."'

R Whites was set up in 1845 by Robert and Mary White, who sold home-brewed ginger beer from a barrow in Camberwell. But their descendants would have to wait another 128 years until the helpful invention of TV, fridges and stripy, pink pyjamas meant the name 'R White' could finally enter the realms of advertising history. The 'Secret Lemonade Drinker' campaign was born in 1973 when actor Julian Chagrin (a presenter on the BBC children's show *Vision On*) tip-toed down the stairs in the middle of the night in a pair of pyjamas, opened the fridge door, grabbed a bottle of R Whites and burst into the title song – just before his wife catches him at it. 'I'm a secret lemonade drinker. I've been trying to give it up but it's one of those nights,' he sings (or rather *Ross MacManus* sings).

MacManus was a jazz musician in the Joe Loss Orchestra who could also do a pretty good Elvis Presley impression and had just recorded an album of Elvis cover versions. MacManus and his teenage son were to play an even larger part in another ad for R Whites. 'We went down to a "cave" in Wardour Street. I took my son, Declan Patrick MacManus. We were meant to be in a club and the idea was that there was no better drink to quench your thirst than R Whites Lemonade.' Again, McManus and his band provided the vocals and musical accompaniment for Julian Chagrin, who was seen fronting a band called The Thirst, in between dashing off stage for sips of lemonade.

Pop history now recalls it was the first television appearance of teenager Declan MacManus, who played guitar and sang backing vocals – but it wouldn't be the last. Four years later he would be on *Top of the Pops* with a number one song called *Oliver's Army,* under his adopted name, Elvis Costello. Though popular at the time in playgrounds the length and breadth of Britain, these two R Whites ads with their distinctive jingle hardly gave any clues to the high esteem in which they would come to be held by *thirtysomethings* 20 years down the line. Indeed, Julian Chagrin gave up the part of the Secret Lemonade Drinker after just a few ads and was last heard of living on a kibbutz. Another actor, Julian Dutton, took on the part. Over the years, the R Whites campaign (probably due to its annoyingly unforgettable song) has taken on cult status – even Sir Paul McCartney once confessed to liking it.

In the eighties a Secret Lemonade Drinkers' club was formed in Leeds. Club members would go on outings with a lemonade theme and play football in *Chagrinesque* pink pyjamas. There were even reports of a Secret Lemonade Drinker handicap race at Lingfield Park. In 1991 another ad agency took on the account and began another R Whites campaign featuring celebrities like John McEnroe, Nicholas Parsons and Ronnie Corbett.

Seven years later the Secret Lemonade Drinker theme was revived for a radio advertising campaign. But, over 25 years on, it's still that manchild creeping down the stairs, while avoiding the sleeping dog, that sticks in the memory. 'I cannot think of this advert without smiling. I don't know why; I don't know what it was about it,' says TV presenter and former *Smash Hits* editor Kate Thornton. 'It really worked. I wish it was still on telly. I'd love to meet the guy from the advert, just to say: "Why *those* pyjamas?"'.

6 LEVI'S 501S
LAUNDERETTE 1985

The opening bars of Marvin Gaye's hit *I Heard It Through The Grapevine* are among the most evocative in television advertising history. For a whole generation, at least, those first few moody seconds only bring one image to mind – that of model Nick Kamen walking into a launderette. The ad might not have been set in the eighties (more likely a mythical fifties), but for many those first few seconds can evoke memories of an entire decade. But Kamen (who only got the part on condition he lost weight) wasn't the first to get his kit off in a launderette. An early Hamlet ad showed a bowler-hatted, be-suited gent undressing in front of a group of women and sticking his clothes, and even his hat, in a washing machine. Sadly, no one remembers the actor's name. And, as far as we know, he never had a hit single written for him by Madonna.

Kamen's 'Launderette' was shown for the first time on Boxing Day 1985. Thought up by John Hegarty and Barbara Noakes of Bartle Bogle Hegarty, the ad campaign was designed to try and save Levi's flagging fortunes; the company was under attack from all sorts of other fashionable brands. In short, Levi's (which had been going since the 1850s) were becoming the sort of jeans worn by people's dads. And not even trendy dads – it was middle-aged 'fuddy duddies' wearing 'Polyester Levi's Action Slacks'.

Research showed that the *intended* target audience for Levi's 501s – 15- to 19-year-olds – saw the United States of the fifties and sixties as a cool time and place in history. James Dean, Elvis Presley and Sam Cooke all belonged to this mythical, wondrous world. Unless the ad agencies came up with something new, the alternative was going with the American campaign for 501s, which was all about how well the jeans fitted in the United States of Ronald Reagan and MOR music. The image seemed the opposite of MTV and European chic.

So, director Roger Lyons was given the go-ahead to film an ad that showed drop dead gorgeous model Nick Kamen stripping down to his boxer shorts, while flustered women and bemused elders looked on, and then sitting and waiting while his jeans were in the wash. All this and Marvin Gaye thrown in too. (Except it wasn't actually Marvin Gaye but a newly recorded 'session' version of the song – though the original was later re-released off the back of the ad and entered the charts all over again.)

'Grapevine' was the first of four Levi's-related songs to all make the Top Ten, a feat that made advertisers realise that choosing the right music was of paramount importance because it really could help push a product on TV. They call it 'integrated marketing' – and it meant a single in the charts and an ad on the box simultaneously, as well as the '501' logo alongside the artist's name on the record sleeve in every record shop in Britain.

Kate Thornton was a schoolgirl at the time and remembers the effect that Kamen's striptease had on her. 'I remember hearing that the ad was running at a cinema before a movie – and I hadn't seen it on the telly at that point. So I went to the cinema just to see the ad,' she says. 'The commercial made those jeans sexy at a time when Levi's were struggling to make their product appealing to women of my age – and really that's where the big spenders come from. Suddenly those jeans became a must-have item. I only wanted them because Nick Kamen wore them and took them off.'

Thornton wasn't the only British teenager to feel that way – consumers wrote in to Levi's in their thousands asking for pictures of Kamen. Meanwhile, sales of 501s shot up by an incredible 800 per cent in the wake of the ad, which eventually had to be taken off the air because the company couldn't produce enough jeans to meet the new demand. By 1987 sales of Levi's jeans were reported to be 20 times what they had been just three years earlier. The commercial also boosted sales of boxer shorts to a record high – though the ad agency only put Kamen in a pair of boxers because they weren't allowed to show their hero in a pair of jockeys. And it wasn't just teenage girls buying the jeans – and with it a little bit of Nick Kamen; boys too were impressed by what Kamen could do. 'The ad said: "Wear Levi's jeans and you'll be a rebel without a cause," says psychologist Dr David Lewis. "You'll be able to alienate older people – who young people despise anyway – and you can be cool."'

Inevitably, Nick Kamen was suddenly flavour of the month. Madonna wrote a song for him called *Each Time You Break My Heart* which made it into the Top Ten. Kamen was soon a fully-fledged pop star – but his new career was short lived. Subsequent singles failed and Kamen moved to Los Angeles where he was to live for a time with British television presenter Amanda de Cadenet. 'There wasn't life for Nick Kamen after Levi's because he broke the rule – he talked,' says Thornton. 'We just liked looking at him. It was as simple as that. He was a model and he just had these smouldering beautiful looks...but fundamentally he was to be looked at and lusted over – and never to be taken seriously.'

Poor old Nick. He turned a new Levi's ad into a much-hyped media event and ended up eventually being replaced in 1999 by a fluffy yellow puppet called Flat Eric. Eric also released a hit single – but didn't get to live with Amanda de Cadenet.

5 BODDINGTONS
MELANIE SYKES **1996**

'The best ads are the ones that play with our preconceptions and take and turn them around,' says Philip Dodd, director of the Institute of Contemporary Arts. The Boddingtons campaign of the late nineties is a perfect example. In turning expectation on its head, it took a traditional Northern bitter and made it into something which felt both sexy and sophisticated. Prior to 1996, comedian Frankie Howerd was among the personalities who had promoted Boddingtons – a beer which had been brewed since 1779 – and had been, just a few years earlier, a regional bitter in decline. Then the ad agency Bartle Bogle Hegarty held an audition for models to star in a new Boddingtons commercial.

A 25-year-old model from the North West was among those who went along and were required to deliver the punchline of the ad the agency was about to make. 'I'd never had to speak to camera before because usually on commercial castings it's for body cream or shampoo – so you just have to do the motions,' recalls Melanie Sykes. 'I just gave it the deepest Northern accent I could pull out – and everyone in the room just cracked up laughing.' Sykes had done other TV ads before – for everything from cars to toothpaste – but Sykes and Boddingtons had something in common which made them a perfect match – both were from Manchester. There was, however, one vital difference – a pint of bitter had an ageing, working-class image; Sykes was young and glamorous. She got the job.

Sykes filmed 'Mansion', her first ad for Boddingtons, which was a spoof on a black and white Clavin Klein **Obsession** ad – in and around a huge house in Malibu. 'I remember seeing Nick Nolte [the American actor] on the first morning, walking his dog and I thought: "Oh my God, we are in Malibu, I can't believe it!"' she recalls. 'I had half-naked men walking round all day – these gorgeous models and me in a white flowy dress. It was like a dream come true.'

The ad worked because sophistication was the last thing you expected in a beer ad – a million miles from Arkwright, his performing dog and John Smith's Bitter. There was also the shock element. At the end of the ad, Sykes points out to the hunk posing in front of her – 'Hey, Torquil, are those trolleys [underpants] on the right way round?' Torquil grunts as he tries to take a look at himself. The Mancunian dialogue is the last thing you would expect from such a glamorous-looking creature (since the demise of Coronation Street's Bet Lynch, anyway).

The ad was directed by Daniel Kleinman, who had shot over 100 pop videos for artists like Madonna and Prince, as well as the Jack Dee penguin ad for John Smith's, and the Harry Enfield spoof documentary about the DJs 'Smashie and

Nicie'. Kleinman later revealed that his aim was to make stunning images that pushed pretentiousness to the edge of credulity – without revealing the end joke.

The ad made an immediate difference to the image of Manchester (where the ad was cheered in pubs whenever it came on TV) as well as the fortunes of Boddingtons and, of course, to Melanie Sykes' career. 'About a week after it came on air I started to get phone calls from TV companies. I remember saying to my model agent "I'm 26 years old, I can't model forever. I might as well go for these things".' And go she did – guest presenting on holiday shows, presenting the *Smash Hits Poll Winners Party* and eventually co-presenting Channel Four's *The Big Breakfast* – all this off the back of one ad. In the middle of all this, Sykes repeated her commercial success in a second ad for Boddingtons. Again it was a spoof – this time based on a Pirelli tyres ad starring Carl Lewis – and was set in the Californian desert.

We see a muscular man sprinting through the sands when suddenly an ice cream van appears and serves up a pint of Boddingtons for the thirsty athlete. 'Do you want a flake in that, love?' asks Sykes, by now known as 'the body of Boddies'. 'Ta,' he replies, in another unexpected bout of Mancunian dialogue. The appearance of ice cream in a Boddingtons ad was not unplanned. The company's press campaign had, for several years, concentrated on the beer's smoothness, shown by a 'creaminess' in a series of ads that were all black and white, apart from the gold of the beer. After all, the drink was known as 'The Cream of Manchester'. Melanie Sykes now divides her time between presenting on TV and radio. But although Sykes replaced many other 'Boddington women' the company found *her* hard to replace. Today's face of Boddies isn't a model but a cartoon cow called Graham Heffer, with the catchphrase 'Waa-hey!'

4 ELECTRICITY ASSOCIATION
HEAT ELECTRIC **1990**

In 1990 Channel Four ran an animated short called *Creature Comforts,* featuring clay models of animals talking about their conditions in a zoo. However, the voices weren't those of the animation equivalent of Johnny Morris; they were provided by *real* people – recorded by the director, Nick Park, in schools, bedsits and old people's homes – and even some vox popped in the street. It gave the animals a human touch that *Animal Magic* could have but dreamed of. *Creature Comforts* was an instant success – winning the 1990 Academy Award for Best Short Animated Film after beating Park's other effort – Wallace and Gromit in *A Grand Day Out.* Soon, the film-makers, Aardman Animations, were inundated with ideas for turning *Creature Comforts* into an ad campaign.

After much thought they decided to go with a campaign for the Electricity Board. 'GGK, an agency in London, came to us with an idea that seemed a step forward,' recalls Park. 'Rather than animals just talking about a product, it was pets in the home – which seemed a very suitable setting.'

Nick Park was born in 1958, the third of five kids. His dad was a photographer and his mum was a tailor. Park went to school in Preston, Lancashire, where he dreamt of emulating the animators that had produced his favourite children's TV shows like *The Clangers* and *Rhubarb and Custard.* Park joined Bristol-based Aardman Animation in 1985 fresh from art school in Sheffield and the National Film and Television School. Just a few years later he would be picking up his first Oscar – and a CBE – for his adventures featuring the clay model Yorkshireman Wallace and his faithful hound, Gromit.

Back in the eighties Aardman was a young but forward-thinking company, founded in 1972 by Peter Lord and David Sproxton, which had started off by producing the children's TV character Morph. Aardman then broke out into the world of pop videos – including memorable animated promos for Peter Gabriel's *Sledgehammer* and Nina Simone's re-released *My Baby Just Cares For Me.* But *Creature Comforts* was perhaps the first sign that big, big things were on the horizon for Aardman – and now the short was to evolve into an advertising campaign that would make the company's work familiar to the entire TV nation. For the 'Heat Electric' campaign Park took up his microphone and tape recorder once again and conducted a series of interviews with people who lived near the Bristol based Aardman Studio, asking them about their use of electricity.

Park then took his tapes back to the studio and constructed 14 ads around the conversations he'd had with everyday folk – put into the mouths of animals seen in

the kitchen and their living rooms. Perhaps the best-loved character of all was Frank the jogging tortoise, complete with headband, who liked an electric shower after a run out. '[For that] I went to this guy called Frank who lives in Bristol,' recalls Park 'and he just came out with some fantastic phrases which were completely without thinking – like "turn off and onable". I thought that was a gem really, and I don't think anyone could have written that in a million years, it was so perfect.'

Everyone loved the originality of the ads and the way that they personified animals – especially because they personified them into normal-sounding people with regional accents. Some of the characters even came over as shy and introverted – which Park thinks was unusual in an advertising campaign. There was only one problem. The public seemed to have difficulty remembering what those fantastic new ads were for. 'Everyone thought they were for gas. People still refer to them as "the gas adverts", says Park, whose first feature film, *Chicken Run (co-directed with Aardman co-founder Peter Lord)*, opened to public and critical acclaim in early 2000.

3 TANGO
ORANGE MAN 1992

The third most popular commercial in *The 100 Greatest TV Ads* was a real slap in the face for advertising – well, for soft drink advertising anyway. Prior to the Tango campaign most ads for soft drinks showed kids drinking the stuff. This piece of classic advertising slapstick didn't have any kids drinking Tango in it, but it did have someone that looked like a great, big, orange baby.

The ad came at a critical period in Tango's 40-year-existence, as Rupert Howell, chairman of the ad agency HHCL, explains: 'Tango was a very big but static and dusty brand...miles and miles behind Coke and Pepsi. The way we described it at the time was that it was a can of Tango which would be gathering dust on the back of a warm fish and chip shop shelf; it was very unfashionable. What we did in a period of less than three months was turn it from that into a youth icon.' Art director Trevor Robinson and his copywriter partner Al Young were given the job of turning Tango's fortunes around. 'Before we got the business the Tango ads were just this very urban street thing – like kids washing the windscreens of cars which had stopped at traffic lights,' says Young. '[They had] something at the end about: "You can beat the clock but you can't beat the taste of our orange juice" – something like that. It was, in my opinion, very bad youth advertising,' says Young.

Young and Robinson decided to change the formula by doing a mickey take of the sorts of coffee ads which were popular at the time where, according to Young, 'someone would take a drink of coffee and go: "Wow, that's great coffee!." We just took that whole idea of exaggerating the moment to a real stupid extreme,' adds Robinson. 'It sort of came out of American football really.' The pair had been keen followers of the sport on Channel Four and noticed the use of close tactical analysis. Indeed, they thought it was something they could use in an advertising campaign. So they dreamt up an action replay scenario, which they shot on Chiswick High Street, showing a big, orange man coming out of nowhere and slapping (Eric and Ernie-like, according to Robinson) a young man on the cheeks when he takes a sip of Tango.

The slap had started off as a punch before it was toned down, and was meant to demonstrate 'the hit of real oranges'; the makers of Tango were proud to boast that they used real orange juice in their product. In fact, the original plans were to have an American sports commentator doing the voices – but it was decided that American voices were inappropriate for a British brand. Instead, the agency used former footballer and pundit Ray Wilkins to comment *Match of the Day* replay style

on the actions of the orange man: 'The big orange fella runs on from the left and gives him a good old slappin,' says Wilkins. Young and Robinson also tried out darts commentator Sid Waddell – but ended up using comedy actor Hugh Dennis who they reckoned sounded more like Sid than Waddell himself.

Meanwhile, the orange man was played by an actor called Peter Geeves, who had passed an unusual audition. 'We just got in lots of big, fat men who were bald and painted them orange,' says Young. 'It was the way he moved, as well,' adds Robinson. 'He defied his size. He was a massive guy but he had this fast little run.'

With its action replays and spoof sports commentary, the ad tapped into two important subjects – the growth in popularity of TV sport and, with it, the use of video technology. It also set a style of low-budget, hand-held camera commercials that were to become popular as the nineties moved on. The ad ended with the words: 'You know when you've been Tango'd' – delivered by singer-songwriter Gil Scott Heron who the pair had just seen in concert at the Jazz Café in Camden, North London.

All was going well until, after a few days of the ad going out, *The Sun* printed a story about school kids copying the orange man's violent slap. 'It sparked a playground craze. People used to go round slapping people, saying: "You've been Tango'd," says Rupert Howell. Howell even recalls taking a phone call from a surgeon, who said: 'Look, I'm not the complaining type but I thought you'd like to know I did an operation on a child this morning with a perforated ear drum. As I was wheeling him into the operating theatre I asked him what had happened and he said "I got Tango'd".' The ad agency immediately withdrew the ad before a ban by the authorities could take place, and replaced the slap with the orange man kissing his victim.

All in all, it didn't make much difference to an already popular campaign. It was reported that this one commercial had boosted the sales of Tango by 300 per cent and made it the third bestselling brand of soft drink after Coca Cola and Pepsi.

 SMASH
MARTIANS **1973**

Cadbury's wasn't the first company to use visitors from another planet to sell their wares on British television. That honour goes to Blue Car Travel who won industry awards in 1961 for an ad starring future *Sale of The Century* presenter Nicholas Parsons and his wife Denise Bryer as two aliens who don't speak our lingo. But the Smash Martians got the last laugh. They laughed a lot in fact. It was their 'catchphrase' and a permanent feature of a campaign which dominated TV advertising in the early seventies.

This most popular of campaigns came out of a conversation in a London pub between BMP art director John Webster and his writer colleague Chris Wilkins. Cadbury's had just bought Smash from a Canadian company and was looking for a new way of selling the instant imitation potato – and in the process hopefully outselling their rivals Wonder Mash and Yeoman. But how on earth could they make a bowl of mashed potato look appetising on television? After all, other ad agencies had tried with Smash and found the task difficult. Remembering that chat in the pub, Webster says: 'I said [to Chris]: "If an alien came from another planet and saw someone bothering to clean up a potato, peel it, boil it for 20 of their

minutes, mash it all up and then put it on a plate – when they can just pour hot water on a powder and serve it – they'd think they were mad.'"

From that developed a script for a one-off ad – with which Cadbury's were not impressed. They favoured a campaign that was more serious about the nutritional benefits of Smash. In the end both ads were made – and put out to research. 'Nobody remembered the nutritional, worthy ads but they laughed like hell at the aliens,' says Webster.

The Smash Martians (or 'heavy metal chimps', as someone once described them) were introduced to the British public in 1973 (pre-dating space-age *Star*

Wars) with voices supplied by Peter Hawkins who had also been the voice of Dr Who's arch enemies, the Daleks. The first ads showed a gathering of martians around a table doing just what Webster and Wilkins (during that fateful pub conversation) had imagined them to do. 'First they peel them with their metal knives…then they boil them for 20 minutes…they are clearly a most primitive people,' says the lead alien.

The martians were three-foot high models on a platform, each worked by three operators who sat underneath them, using levers to move their arms, heads and bodies. 'The director, Bob Brooks, was well-known for being short-tempered,' says Webster. 'He used to let fly at the martians and say: "What the hell are you doing at the back? Will you pay attention?" It was very funny to see this sort of relationship between the director and these tin things.' Indeed, set designer David Bill explains how the martians' famous, infectious laugh was as a result of the American director's attitude. 'Bob had a lot to say for himself, being American!' says Bill. 'All the puppeteers were taking the mick. They had all these puppets lying around in their space ship and they were sort of talking in American voices and doing jokes – and they started to make them laugh. I said: "That's great! We should do that."'

The ads for instant potato were an instant success – so much so that the martians started getting fan mail from TV viewers, intrigued by these funny, strange beings from outer space who (in the ads that followed) were part of some extraterrestrial family. 'They wanted to know where they came from…and children particularly wanted to know the stories,' says Webster. 'We brought out four books about the martian families and their adventures, which sold in the shops.' The ad agency BMP was even approached by television companies who were keen on giving the martians their own series – but Cadbury's didn't want to proceed with the idea. One of the most memorable components of the initial eight-year Smash Martian campaign was its theme tune – 'For Mash Get Smash'. Yet here was a jingle born very much out of simplicity. 'We went to see Cliff Adams who was the top jingle writer at the time,' says Webster. 'We walked in the room and he was sitting in the corner [at the piano] and I said we wanted some kind of jingle for "For Mash Get Smash". Before I'd finished the sentences he went: "How about this?" What he played was perfect. In a mini-second he'd done something which ran for ten years and he got money for it every time it was played.'

Nearly 30 years on, the martians have been revived for the third time in ten years – and are still doing the business for Cadbury's. Smash still has a more than healthy share of the market – even if these advertising icons seem as intrinsically seventies as David Cassidy, bell-bottom trousers and the platform shoe.

1 GUINNESS
SURFER **1999**

'Good things come to those who wait'. So goes the slogan, anyhow, at the end of the commercial that picked up more votes than any other in *The 100 Greatest TV Ads*. The public decided that Guinness (or one of its latest ads, at least) really was 'good for you'. Perhaps there is, as some people have said, an element of the 'now' about the vote – people voting for the most recent ad that they love. But there's no doubt that 'Surfer' *will* go down in history as a classic ad; the fact that it was recently voted the best ad of 1999 is testament to that.

Guinness is a company with an impressive history in British advertising. The first newspaper ads for the stout first appeared in the UK in 1929 and Guinness ads have been making waves ever since. 'Guinness is good for you' was the original slogan, but a tightening up of what advertisers could say led to its disappearance, replaced by confusing slogans like 'Guinless isn't good for you' and 'Tall, dark and have some'. In the eighties and nineties the slogans evolved into 'Pure Genius' and 'Not everything in black and white makes sense'. It's fitting (for an ad voted the greatest of all time) that Guinness was around at the very beginning – advertised

alongside Gibbs SR on the first night of ITV in 1955 in a spot showing a seal getting away with a zoo-keeper's Guinness. But unlike Heineken, John Smith's Bitter and Carling Black Label, Guinness' TV campaigns up until the nineties haven't stood the test of time as well – though the 1987 campaign featuring blonde haired actor Rutger Hauer dressed all in black was a popular one, and was reshot with different actors for different audiences all over the world.

Director Tony Kaye turned Guinness TV ads into an art form in 1996, working off the slogan: 'Not everything in black and white makes sense'. His commercial memorably ended on a shot of a fish riding a bicycle along a promenade before we read the words 'A woman needs a man like a fish needs a bicycle.' Three years later director Jonathan Glazer picked up the artistic baton, working on an ad which he later said was 'like filming an avalanche...houses coming down'.

'Surfer' was created by Tom Carty and Walter Campbell of ad agency Abbott Mead Vickers BBDO. As seems to be the case with many classic ads, the inspiration for the ad came from the local pub. 'We worked out that it took 120 seconds to pour a pint of Guinness and then wait for it to settle,' says Carty. 'Going right back to the forties [there was the line] "Guinness is good for you"...we kind of combined that with the [waiting] time and you get: "Good things come to those who wait."

Carty and Campbell had just worked on a previous Guinness ad about an Italian swimmer and were keen to return to the water with a surfing ad that drew a parallel with the wait for a pint of Guinness to settle and a surfer's wait for the perfect wave. However, both were cautious of approaching a subject whose popular connotations involved Old Spice and the Beach Boys.

Fresh inspiration came from the movie *Moby Dick* and paintings by Eugène Delacroix and Walter Crane which showed white horses mingling with waves. The ad agency combined the image of the horse with the surfing theme – and several months later, in January 1999, set off for Hawaii to film it.

'A real Polynesian surfer waiting for the most amazing surf of his life – that's what it is,' says Carty, summing up the plot in one sentence. 'Then it becomes what's in his mind's eye. The horses become symbolic because they become the experience of riding a 60ft wave.'

Jonathan Glazer takes up the story of how they cast the part of the surfers. 'We didn't want the perfect face. We wanted people who looked like they would genuinely wait for this extraordinary wave – and only *they* would know when it was going to come.' Glazer and his team scoured the local islands, looking at nearly 300 surfers, but they eventually found the 'star' of their ad in unusual circumstances. 'We found him under a palm tree on a beach. He was just a beach bum living out there who surfed for the female tourists,' recalls Glazer. When Glazer had picked another three (more accomplished) local surfers, filming could begin on a Hawaiian beach where Polynesians kings are said to be buried. 'We had umpteen experts on the end of the phone, telling us where the waves were expected and where various sets [of waves] were going to come – it was unplannable as a shoot really.' It was also a dangerous shoot over eight days – not so much for Glazer who issued instructions from a speedboat – but for the main surfer, who Glazer admits looked terrified by the ordeal, as he was far from an expert.

It would make his accomplishment of surfing the big wave feel even more satisfying. It was also pretty hairy for the cameramen who filmed the surfers while hanging off the edge of the boat. Sometimes, washed off the vessel, they would be in the water for several minutes before they could get picked up. Glazer sets the scene: 'You are travelling along on a boat, you've got a camera hanging off the back and there's a 50ft wall of water moving towards you at 60mph or 70mph – and you are trying to get your shot. It's quite phenomenal.' Once the team had completed filming in Hawaii they then had the difficult job of combining the surfers (who had been pictured waiting for, surfing and then celebrating the perfect wave) with the white horses – who were to be filmed in a studio in England.

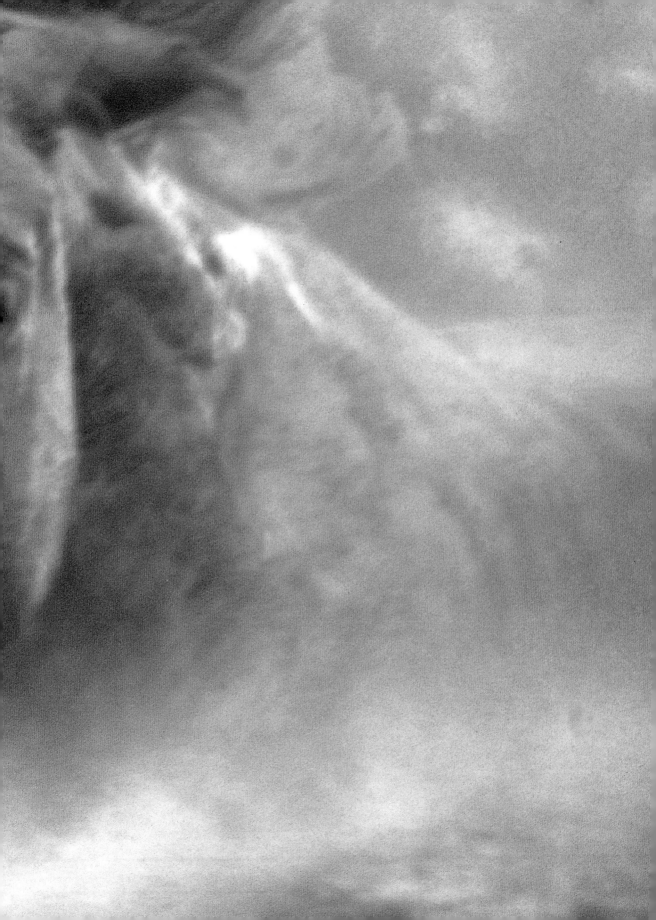

GOOD THINGS COME TO THOSE WHO...

Glazer used Lippizaner horses and had them painted with muscle tone so that their muscle definition would show up on film. He shot them again and again over three days jumping over fences until he was sure that, by using state-of-the-art computer technology, the two shoots would match up. But if anything, this was even more difficult than filming the surfers. 'There was a time – right up to the last week or so – that we weren't going to have the horses,' says Glazer. 'There was a time when we looked at each other and thought: "Do we really need them?" Thankfully, they came out as well as they did.'

All that was left to do was to add the now familiar soundtrack. Originally, the ad agency wanted to use excerpts from the radio version of *Under Milk Wood,* read by Richard Burton – all put to an instrumental track by the group Leftfield. But the client didn't think it would work. So Tom Carty and Walter Campbell had to come up with new prose. They went back to the story of Ahab in *Moby Dick* and came up with a commentary starting off with: 'He waits that's what he does. And I'll tell you what. Tick follows tock follows tick follows tock". The last line was influenced by a James Joyce novel but was also a reference to the time spent waiting for a pint of Guinness to settle. As we hear these words (read by a drinking pal of Glazer's, called Louie) the camera concentrates for an unusually long time on the face of the main surfer, whose eyes appear to be pointing in different directions. It is an enthralling and disconcerting opening gambit. How could anyone not continue to watch to see what happens? Indeed, how could anyone take their eyes off the TV screen right through to the unusually silent celebration on the beach at the end of the ad, 60 seconds later?

TV presenter and former *Smash Hits* editor Kate Thornton was one of millions impressed by the commercial. 'I don't know a single person – and I'm talking from my parents' friends right down to 14, 15-year-olds – who weren't impressed by that ad,' she says. 'It helped to reposition Guinness in my mind. Fifteen years ago Guinness was a drink that you associated with men who just drank themselves into a stupor until they were vomiting into a pool on the floor. Now suddenly, on the back of the ad, it's become incredibly chic...It became a rather sophisticated product by association – and that's a really clever thing to do.'

The Surfer ad is just about the most expensive ad in the Top 100 – if not *the* most expensive. As to how much it cost, no one seems prepared to say – though estimates of £1 million wouldn't be far off the mark.

But no one can argue that it wasn't good value for money. From the beach of Polynesian kings, the king of British ads.

BIBLIOGRAPHY

The 100 Best TV Commercials – Bernice Kanner – Random House, 1999
The Tuppeny Punch and Judy Show – Jo Gable – Michael Joseph, 1980
20th Century Advertising – Dave Saunders – Carlton Books, 1999
Campaign Hall of Fame – Haymarket Publishing, 1999
The Commercials Book – Peter Etterdgui and Paul Kemp Robertson – British
    Design and Art Direction, 1997
You Got An Ology? – Maureen Lipman and Richard Phillips – Robson Books, 1989
British Television Advertising – the First 30 Years – Brian Henry – Century
Benham, 1996

**Advertising Effectiveness Awards – papers published by the Institute of
Practitioners in Advertising (IPA):**
Angus Fear, Allen Brady Marsh, 1990 – Tango
Pamela Vick and Mo Fisher, Leo Burnett, 1982 – Flake
Guy Murphy, Bartle Bogle Hegarty, 1994 – Boddingtons
Hilary Boszko, D'Arcy Macmanus Benton and Bowles, 1990 – Tetley Tea
Michael Ellyatt, Publicis, 1996 – Renault Clio
John Carter, WCRS, 1994 – Carling Black Label
Giles Lury and Paul Hackett, J Walter Thompson, 1992 – Oxo
Clive Cooper, Louise Cook and Nigel Jones, BMP DDB Needham – PG Tips
E Thomas, J Walter Thompson, 1986 – Andrex
Mary Stow, Paul Baker and Terry Prue, 1992 – Andrex
Tim Lindsay, Bartle Bogle Hegarty, 1988 – Levi's
Stephen Walker, Bartle Bogle Hegarty, 1992 – Levi's
Gareth John, Foote Cone and Belding, 1982 – Turkish Delight
Colin Flint, McCann Erickson, 1996 – Gold Blend

OTHER SOURCES
An Analysis of the Energizer Bunny Commercial Sequence by Amam J Smargon
Fred the Homepride Man internet site by Jennifer Woodward:
www.collectiques.net/collectables/july1998/homepride_fred.htm

PICTURE CREDITS